Removing the Ring of Submission

REMOVING *the* RING *of* SUBMISSION

EXPOSING THE TRUTH ABOUT OSTEOPATHY AND ITS MEDICAL MYSTICISM

KAREN MELTON, PHYSICIAN

XULON PRESS

Xulon Press
2301 Lucien Way #415
Maitland, FL 32751
407.339.4217
www.xulonpress.com

© 2019 by Karen Melton, Physician

Edited by Xulon Press

All rights reserved solely by the author. The author guarantees all contents are original and do not infringe upon the legal rights of any other person or work. No part of this book may be reproduced in any form without the permission of the author. The views expressed in this book are not necessarily those of the publisher.

Unless otherwise indicated, Scriptures are taken from the New Revised Standard Version Catholic Edition (NRSVCE) New Revised Standard Version Bible: Catholic Edition, copyright © 1989, 1993 the Division of Christian Education of the National Council of the Churches of Christ in the United States of America. Used by permission. All rights reserved.

Printed in the United States of America.

ISBN-13: 978-1-5456-8047-6

Disclaimer:

This book does not represent medical or spiritual advice. You are encouraged to speak to someone you trust in interpreting and understanding the contents of this book. I am not responsible for your choices or actions.

This book was written with the purpose of finding the truth. This book was written to shine a light on the osteopathic tenets and practice. This book represents my opinion of the tenets and my experience of the osteopathic paradigm including its practice. This book represents what I have learned about paradigms and their effects on our choices, behavior, and mental states.

This book represents what I have learned about the nature of our spiritual selves and the spiritual world. This book was written from my Christian/Catholic perspective. It in no way represents any official opinion from any person, church, or group. These are my beliefs in the unseen. They are my beliefs as to what the tenets claim about the unseen, the mystical. I make no authoritative claim to the accuracy of any spiritual or philosophical discussion made in the book. Though I stand by and believe that what I have said is true regarding the osteopathic philosophy and mysticism, I make no claim in knowing all, seeing all, and understanding all. I make no claims on understanding the totality of you, the universe, or any metaphysical reality. As it should be, you have to discover for yourself what is true and what truth is.

The World Psychiatric Association (WPA) in conjunction with the World Health Organization (WHO) put out a position paper regarding religion/spirituality. They list religion/spirituality as a part of a quality of life. They also state that, "Psychiatrists should be knowledgeable concerning the potential for both benefit and harm of religious, spiritual and secular worldviews and practices and be willing to share this information in a critical but impartial way with the wider community in support of the promotion of health and well-being." This statement, my faith, and my conscience have guided me in writing this book.

I have stated the facts as to what I have found to be amiss in the osteopathic paradigm to the best of my knowledge and ability. I possess no degree in physics, psychology, philosophy, or theology. I regret if I have inadvertently stated or misrepresented anything in any way in this book.

No names have been used out of respect for the privacy of others.

I have included letters, e-mails, and papers that I have written and sent to the American Osteopathic Association (AOA) and their representatives. They have been minimally amended. Some have been shortened when needed, corrected for errors, and grammatically changed as I removed names.

This book in no way is a critique of the allopathic profession or the allopathic portion of osteopathic training. This book is about my desire to remove myself from anything osteopathic and retain solely my allopathic training.

Table of Contents

Preface ix

Introduction–Overview xiii

Chapter 1 – Wellness, the New Wooden Idol 1

Chapter 2 – The Tenets, the Osteopathic Whole, Holism, and Anatomy: Putting it all Together 9

Chapter 3 – The Appeal Process 19

Chapter 4 – Holistic Healthcare from a Torah Perspective: Idolatry, Generic Spirituality, Marketing of the Metaphysical ... 35

Chapter 5 – Scope of Practice: Is Osteopathy a Religion? 43

Chapter 6 – Possession Medicine: Biodynamics of Osteopathy in the Cranial Field 53

Chapter 7 – Scams and Cults, Wolves in Sheep's Clothes 61

Conclusion 69

PREFACE

Osteopathy needs a strike.

Senator B. read over my stuff, sat me down in his office, and the first words out of his mouth were, "When did you know you were in a cult?" (The word cult was not mentioned in my writing.) I said, "It took me twelve years, it took you ten minutes."

Whenever I state the facts about osteopathic philosophy and practice, some sort of initial gut reaction is evoked. One former prosecutor, quipped, "Sounds like mind control to me." Another friend said, "This sounds like a religion." One of my osteopathic students blurted out, "This should be taught in a church." After twelve years in the profession followed by nine years studying the philosophy, I can tell you that there is validity to these responses. In order for you to make up your own mind, however, we have to talk about the osteopathic Tenets, the core of the philosophy. We have to dissect every word and we have to look at where those words take us.

Reliving this makes me feel a little like Bilbo or Frodo Baggins writing their memoirs, *There and Back Again, A Hobbit's Tale*. This is a Catholic's tale, a Catholic's perspective. This is the account of how I went into medical school a Catholic, a monotheist, believing in the one true God, was indoctrinated into an organization with many negative cult-like behaviors, formed into an osteopath, unknowingly believed the tenets, put on a ring of submission so to speak, to the osteopathic paradigm, and became a holistic spiritual practitioner. Osteopathy is a spiritual practice. From a Christian perspective, it is an apostasy. It is a defection, an abandonment of the biblical God. It was only by grace that I found myself safely back home again within Christ, within biblical truth, and within the Catholic Church. This is my *There and Back Again*.

> *"There is no question as to whether there can be a spiritual element within osteopathic medical care," writes one of the representatives of the American Osteopathic Association (AOA). "A core tenet of osteopathic medicine is that: 'The body is a unit; the person is a unit of body, mind, and spirit.' The question has been whether that spiritual element is compatible with your own spirituality and Catholic faith....Theology and spirituality are highly personal. The AOA and I certainly respect whatever decision you reach. However, AOA is dedicated to advancing osteopathic medicine and osteopathic physicians. We are unable to offer you a non-osteopathic credential or give you legal authority to promote yourself as an MD."*

Finally, there was acknowledgement that osteopathy had its own spirituality. This was a happy moment for me reading those words in an e-mail November of 2014. There really is no question. There is and can be a spiritual element in osteopathic medical care. I spent two years trying to get the American Osteopathic Association (AOA) to understand I could not be one of their members because the philosophy and practice of osteopathy was spiritual. By being a member of the AOA and practicing osteopathic principles, I would be violating my own religious beliefs. It was a wonderful moment when they got it. Now the question was, would they accommodate me and find a way for me to renounce osteopathic religious spiritual thought and keep my allopathic/scientific (traditionally called MD) medical training.

Preface

The answer was a resounding no!

The reason, I later discovered, is that the National Board of Osteopathic Medical Examiners (NBOME) has wed that spiritual element to my training, license, and all domains of patient care.

The legal scope of allowed practice **is** the distinct osteopathic spirituality set forth in the Tenets and nothing else. It is through the eyes of the osteopathic Tenets the student and graduate are mandated to practice. Osteopathic certification and licensure reflect/contain the osteopathic spirituality.

> *"Osteopathic physicians must demonstrate knowledge of osteopathic principles and practice such that care of patients is approached from the distinct behavioral, philosophical and procedural aspects of osteopathic medical practice related to the four tenets of osteopathic medicine: 1) the body is a unit; the person is a unit of body, mind, and spirit; 2) the body is capable of self-regulation, self-healing, and health maintenance; 3) structure and function are reciprocally interrelated; and 4) rational treatment is based on an understanding of the basic principles of body unity, self-regulation, and the interrelationship of structure and function."*

I feel I could just end the book right here. The above says it all. Really let this sink in! The beliefs **are** the purview of the practice. For example, if we were talking about the person and the body and an Eastern practice of Chakras, a yoga philosophy with points of spiritual energy, cleansing of the chakras would be their legal scope. They could not bless, they could not say the Our Father or Hail Mary. They could only do what they were trained and licensed to do.

So, by law their representative was right. The AOA could not offer me a non-osteopathic credential. I was an osteopath and all that title entailed including any osteopathic mysticism. My job was to be an osteopath and if it had a spirituality of spirit/body chakras (points of physical or spiritual energy), then by law that is what I would be allowed to do. By law, I was not authorized to bring forth my own spirituality or any other deeply held belief. The osteopathic spirituality legally becomes a part of all domains of patient care. This is what the osteopath is authorized to do. This is what the osteopath is mandated to do.

So, by definition, if you do not believe that you or your patient has a spirit, you are not, nor could you be an osteopath. If you believe you are other than a unit of body, mind, and spirit you could not be an osteopath either.

Religious freedom is gone. Informed consent is never given and the AOA and the NBOME can do what they want which is to promote the osteopathic philosophy.

I am pretty sure this is what the Senator saw right away, though we didn't discuss it. It is called "forced adherence" and is one of the cultic aspects of the osteopathic profession.

To be an osteopath, you must adhere to a set of Tenets or beliefs including the definition of the person and the implications thereof. The Tenets are not up for discussion. They are the creed, the basis for the entire osteopathic profession. You believe them, practice them, and are credentialed for them or not. Hence, you are legally an osteopath or not.

INTRODUCTION

Overview

Throughout this book you will hear from the men and women of Osteopathy as I try to unpack the Tenets for you. Anyone researching and writing about the Tenets cannot overstate their importance. In fact, all philosophies are significant because all thought is significant. The question in a free society becomes, "What will you accept and what will you renounce?" Statements such as body unity, holistic, mind-body-spirit, reciprocally interrelated and self-healing all have profound meaning.

For me, they were meanings disturbing, not life giving, and in direct conflict with my own personal beliefs. They were thoughts that alienated me from God.

Though in plain sight, the Tenets are hidden from the Osteopath. Medical school is so hard; no one I knew had time to read a Tenet. We didn't have a Tenet class. We didn't have Tenet discussions or Tenet lessons. Yet, they are what define the osteopath.

This is another aspect of negative cults. Information is hidden. First you get initiated, and then you get the information. I became aware of the significance of the Tenets three years after completion of my residency when I finally had time to pay attention.

As I tried to extricate myself from the Tenets in an appeal process to the AOA, I kept getting the same response: "You knew and you chose." Well, I didn't know so I did not in fact choose.

In an article in the JAOA (Journal of the American Osteopathic Association) in 2005, one osteopath writes, "The lack of a clear definition of osteopathic medicine and a unifying identity of the osteopathic physician has been labeled the 'paradox of osteopathy.'" This hallmark article was written in response to a challenge put to the osteopathic community to define its reputed distinctiveness.

I would laugh if it wasn't so serious, but the philosophy and Tenets are mandated but not understood. In fact, they are hidden in rhetoric using catch phrases and altruistic language. If the good people of the osteopathic profession understood the meaning of their own Tenets, they wouldn't believe one of them. No one has taken the time to unravel a web of illogic that has been perpetrated on the entire medical world.

Chapter 1

WELLNESS, THE NEW WOODEN IDOL

The following is from the AOA website. Doctrinal confusion is another cult tactic.

Doctors of Osteopathic Medicine or DOs believe there's more to good health than the absence of pain or disease. As guardians of wellness, DOs focus on prevention by gaining a deeper understanding of your lifestyle and environment, rather than just treating your symptoms. It makes a difference when your physician is trained to truly listen. To pay more attention to you than your chart. To look beyond the symptoms and take the time to get to know you as a whole person. Listening to you and partnering in your care are at the heart of our holistic, empathic approach to medicine. We are trained to promote the body's natural tendency toward health and self-healing. We practice according to the latest science and use the latest technology. But we also consider options to complement pharmaceuticals and surgery. There are more than 100,000 DOs in the US, practicing their distinct philosophy in every medical specialty. We have additional training in Osteopathic Manipulative Treatment and use this tool to help diagnose, treat, and prevent illness and injury. We are Doctors of Osteopathic Medicine and the way we practice healthcare is different. We don't see patients. We see people.

Osteopaths want us to believe they are sagacious. (I should know I had that persona for years.) They want us to believe they have a higher kind of insight into us and our medical conditions. But do they? During medical school, our instructors couldn't give some of my classmates the answers they needed so they ran from anything "osteopathic." In fact, one classmate would often say, "I feel like they hand me dog food and expect me to think it is filet mignon." I wish I had been more like my classmates. Unfortunately, I bought into the osteopathic paradigm.

Interestingly, the rhetoric from the AOA has shifted with time. When I started this book, I had no idea that the AOA was adopting the wellness paradigm. But I am not surprised.

Some critics of "wellness" note it is vague; it contains a certain religiosity, is unattainable, and has cult features. I saw one definition of wellness that said, "A condition of change in which the individual moves forward, climbing toward a higher potential of functioning." Another writer said, "It is an actively pursued goal." Then there is the osteopathic claim that your wellness can be *guarded*. From what I have read, wellness is a philosophy, a paradigm, an ideology surrounding an expanded state. Many medical practitioners want us to aspire to this expanded state of "wellness." However, much has been written on it and it is not all good.

In *The False Promises of the Wellness Culture*, Daniela Blei, (from a secular viewpoint and with no mention of osteopathy) documents the 3.7 trillion-dollar global wellness industry and its trappings. She looks at its ideology and does a great job of debunking the wellness myth. She notes that wellness is a philosophy that even promoters say will always be an elusive pursuit. It is a carrot on a stick. It doesn't deliver. It is this perpetual inadequacy that wellness promoters are able to capitalize on.

The tricky thing about wellness is that it seems to have all the pieces, social, psychological, physical, and spiritual. But it is missing one important thing. It is missing life. It is a wooden idol, it has feet, but it cannot walk. It has no life. Wellness is subjective and self-directed. Therefore, in itself it offers no life. It isn't a life-giving state, it is a tormenting state. If we look for a state within ourselves that we produce, we will always be banging our heads against a wall. We will never find it. It is never attained because we can't attain/invent/manufacture life. For the Christian, life is Jesus. He said, "I am the Way, the Truth, and the Life. No one comes to the Father except through me." Wellness to the Christian is another counterfeit Christ. It is another counterfeit Christ trying to get us into a counterfeit kingdom. Or worse, it is another counterfeit Christ trying to get us into the real Kingdom of God through the back door. The latter of which will never happen.

This is serious stuff, but the AOA tosses around philosophies willy-nilly and for what end? I cannot speak to their motives. But the history is there. The wellness paradigm that the AOA has adopted is like a belief that I heard for years. As stated by the founder of osteopathy, Andrew Taylor Still, "Anyone can find disease, but the osteopath can find *'the Health'*." A.T. Still might well have said, "Anyone can find disease, but the osteopath can find *'the Wellness'*." The way that the Health had been used in my training was much like a wellness concept. It also was used as a vital force or an entity. Trying to find these entities or imagine these states left me in a state of despair. I never could find the hidden Health, so I know for sure that I could not find, never mind guard your wellness.

The reason for this, I have come to know, is that wellness/the Health is a state of being geared at replacing God/Life, and the state of being in His Kingdom. Jesus came to us with the mission to proclaim the Kingdom of God, to point us to the Father and His Kingdom. Without us knowing about or desiring the state of God's Kingdom, paradigms like wellness will keep on appearing.

We as humans are rebellious. We want things our way, not God's way. We don't like God's morality, rules, mercy, justice, or commandments. We are afraid to imagine the hope, justice, and goodness He has prepared for us. Wellness, the Health, (and I would add holism) tell the individual they can create their own kingdom, their own reality, their own paradigm. They are their own masters.

I don't know about you, I have tried this and it doesn't work. It is a lonely and dangerous place. Instead, I have turned my life over to God. God is my master for no other reason than I love Him and His creation. I live by His rules not my own because I want to spend eternity with Him. I want a happy eternity, not an eternity of my own making.

"In my Father's house are many mansions. If it were not so, I would have told you. I go to prepare a place for you" (John 14:2). My state, my "estate" is being prepared for me as we speak because He was the first to love. In 1 Corinthians 2:9, it says, "However, as it is written: 'What no eye has seen, what no ear has heard, and what no human mind has conceived'-the things God has prepared for those who love him." The world would be an amazing place if we all could just love God and stop trying to change Him or replace Him.

Wellness, the Health, and holism try to replace God and my union, my existence, my relationship, the deep soul space I have with Him. There is nothing I can do to make it happen, to make it appear or to fabricate it. It is a gift, it is grace. I can't manipulate my environment, drink a smoothie, or do ten push-ups to get it. God's grace is always there. I can only shut the door on it. My beliefs, my thoughts, my attitudes, my behaviors, and my will can pull me away and shut the door. Holism and wellness shut the door. These states removed me from the Kingdom of God. They alienated me from God and left me in despair. Like when Frodo or Bilbo put on the ring, they had a new realm, a new reality, and a new master. My heart changed when I believed in anything osteopathic, my heart changed when I believed in the osteopathic paradigm. My heart changed when I believed my form was reciprocally related to my function. My heart would change if I thought that I could achieve wellness. The Kingdom of God is in my heart and in me. My heart changes for the worse when I believe anything other than the Word of God or what is from God. Just like my heart changes if I live in a state of greed, fear, or revenge. These things then become my master.

Recently, I asked one of our visiting priests from India about holism. As quick as a wink, he said, "Holism robs us/the Christian, of the Spirit, the True Holy Spirit. You see it's one or the other. We cannot serve two masters." He said, "Every generation has to find out that they truly need the Lord, the creator and founder of the way that things truly are. There is no other way. Jesus is the Way."

For me, it is the same with wellness, if I allowed this concept, this state of being into my thoughts; it would rob me of the Kingdom of Heaven. I would be in that mindset. Wellness would be my master. This is why a former prosecutor may have quipped, "Sounds like mind control." Use buzz words, don't really say what you mean, and say it often enough and people follow. I now have a new belief, a new paradigm, a new loop, a new bondage, a new master. Wellness is trickery filled with false promises and myth.

You see Christ, God, is at the very heart of my reality, not wellness, not the Health, not a higher consciousness, not some fabricated state. I believe that the world was made through and for Christ and I am in direct relationship to Him through love. As a Christian, I believe that Jesus is God and that through Him, for Him, and by Him the world was made. Every molecule, every atom was made through Jesus. That means every cell in my body was made through, by, and for God. This is where life exists. This is where living water exists. Jesus Christ is the bearer of the water of life. Everything outside of this for me is death. For me, wellness is death. The osteopathic Health is death.

My job is to become holy and have life, a living relationship with a living God, and then reflect that glory back to God. The pinnacle of living this for the Catholic is the Eucharist; it is the Mass. Jesus couldn't bear to be away from us, so He gave us Himself in the Eucharist. When we (Catholics) receive the Eucharist, the body, blood, soul, and divinity of Jesus at Mass, every aspect of us, every cell in us receives God, Jesus. I receive the goodness of the Lord not some wooden idol. I become holy, I become love, I become Jesus, and I receive His healing power, His healing grace, as I become a part of the living God. Any competing ideology about my body and any false ideology about my health (lower case 'h') lead me down a dangerous path away from God.

Jesus said, "Whatsoever you do to the least of my brothers you do unto me." Whatever you try to assign me, you try to assign God. Trying to impose this concept on me is like trying to impose this concept on God. If there is no wellness of God, there can be no wellness of me. You see, I am truly made in His image and likeness. If God has goodness, I have goodness; if God has mercy, I have mercy. I am made perfect by God. God doesn't need to actively pursue anything. God is and has being and so do I. I don't need or want the AOA's wellness or the osteopathic Health. If you put in wellness, you shut out God. God is now taken out of my medical care.

This is why I could not make such a claim about wellness. Yet, as an osteopath, I would be mandated to make and practice these claims. Wellness isn't science, it is a belief, and it's a paradigm. I am being punished by the AOA if I choose not to believe their claims/paradigms. They hold the allopathic portion, the scientific portion, of my training hostage and in bondage to their beliefs. You see, I believe people are looking for goodness, not wellness. People are looking for the goodness of God, the promises of God, the mercy of God in their lives, not some elusive fantasy that some industry/medical community/fabricator/inventor/word spinner/entrepreneur told us we could attain.

The AOA wants me to give up my beliefs and state of being in union with God, for the wellness state and holistic belief. These are two concepts and states I will never believe are beneficial. Nor should I be required to follow or promote.

As finders of the Health or now, guardians of wellness, the osteopath inflates him or herself and becomes the superhero with super guardian powers needed for God replacement. What damaged me was the belief that God would send these forces and states of being to me and not send Himself. The Health/wellness concepts alienated me from God and His Kingdom and left me feeling even more alone. These concepts replace the reality of God's grace.

The "wellness" industry capitalizes on people striving for something elusive, often through fads and false promises. Yet, the AOA claims they know what it is and will guard it for you.

To further understand the meaning of the Osteopathic philosophy (and what the AOA claims), we have to look seriously at the Tenets. To help us discern the Tenets, we have to go to real philosophers and theologians. I had to go back to my Catholic roots and through that lens I was able to see things clearly. I had to go back to biblical truth. To my knowledge, no one has approached the Tenets in this way. God and the state of His Kingdom have not only been omitted from the Tenets, but discussing the Tenets in relation to the existence of God has not been done.

Saint Augustine said, "You have made us for yourself, O Lord, and our heart is restless until it rests in you." I belong to God and desire to live in God, in His Kingdom, in His divine will, His rules, His laws, and not some fabricated state.

Chapter 2

THE TENETS, THE OSTEOPATHIC WHOLE; HOLISM AND ANATOMY PUTTING IT ALL TOGETHER

If you google Tenet's of Osteopathy, this is what you will find as of April, 2019:

> *Explore the philosophy behind the practice of osteopathic medicine.* DOs are trained to promote the body's natural tendency toward self-healing and health.
>
> ***The Tenets of Osteopathic Medicine express the underlying philosophy of osteopathic medicine and were approved by the AOA House of Delegates as policy.***
>
> *The body is a unit; the person is a unit of body, mind, and spirit.*
>
> *The body is capable of self-regulation, self-healing, and health maintenance.*
>
> *Structure and function are reciprocally interrelated.*
>
> *Rational treatment is based upon an understanding of the basic principles of body unity, self-regulation, and the interrelationship of structure and function.*

If you are a serious philosopher interested in the meaning of every word, you will go away empty-handed. If you believe that your spirit is related to God and can only be spoken about in this context, where is God in all of this? You won't find one word about God because the Tenets have shut Him out. They have created a new spiritual paradigm bereft of God.

What happens when we shut out God? For one thing osteopathic holism happens.

I have to applaud the following osteopathic author because he was trying to identify the distinctiveness of the osteopathic philosophy. Not many have tried to do what he has done. He looks at the holistic concept. In a chapter from an osteopathic text he states, "Holism is the contemporary osteopath's claim." No one would argue with that especially the AOA. He goes on to say that "holism is an acceptance of the totality and indivisibility of a system." That is one way to put it. He states that holism isn't unique to osteopathic thought. That is true. He looks for what is unique to osteopathy and points to "the spinal somatic dysfunction as the focal point for holism."

The somatic dysfunction is an anatomical condition unique to osteopathy. He is saying that this anatomical condition is the cornerstone for holism. It is through this focal point/cornerstone that everything is connected. The author is saying this may be through the spine, a spinal irritation or pathway. Simply put, if you stub your toe and it irritates a spinal segment, it can affect your liver; if you have a kidney cyst it may affect your toe. All of this can happen because of neurons, interneurons, swelling in a spinal segment, etc. (Though I am not well versed in this field, he may be describing reflexology, which to my knowledge has never been proven true.)

Using a tachyarrhythmia (a fast and irregular heart rate) and carpal tunnel syndrome as an example, he proposes a hypothetical link and a hypothetical treatment. As a scientist, he couldn't say, "Let me treat your carpal tunnel syndrome. It will help your tachyarrhythmia (a serious condition)" without proof. So, the author concedes that massive amounts of clinical data would be needed. Obviously, that is an understatement. If you are treating the whole body, if everything is connected, if all is one through the spinal column, or a hormone system, or a fluid milieu, if all is indivisible, that means you must know everything! You must know all! You must know every possibility! Just because there is a little edema here or a little edema there in a spinal segment doesn't mean a thing. You can't forget about every other system in the body, because all is indivisible. You can't forget about what the patient ate in the third grade or how they were brought up. It is all connected, it is all one. The author alludes to this when in his hypothetical example he includes the patient's emotional state.

If you look in the Stanford Encyclopedia of Philosophy, holism is a very broad topic. They describe methodological holism, metaphysical holism, ontological holism, a thesis of non-separability, entangled states, property holism, nomological holism, monism, and quantum and string theory.

"The metaphysical holist believes that the nature of some wholes is not determined by that of their parts," says the encyclopedia. We see this thought in osteopathy, "A lesion is seen as a unit of dysfunction involving the Whole person." And, "Osteopathy isn't about a technique it is a way of treating the whole patient; body, mind, and spirit; the Lot!"

Body, mind, and spirit comprise the whole. Osteopaths propose a metaphysical reality that they are privy to, this is clear. Osteopaths think and make the claim that they can look at your whole, the totality of you. This includes all of the number of variables in you, in your spirit, in your condition, in your illness, in any situation. This is even beyond the scope of any computer because there are an infinite number of possibilities that only an eternal, infinite, omnipotent being can possibly know and see. Only God can have the capabilities that an osteopath/holist is talking about. They elevate themselves to God as does any holistic claim. They elevate themselves to infinite, omnipotent, and eternal.

This gets more in need of scrutiny because the NBOME mandates that I believe and approach my patients with all of the Tenets, not just some form of holism. This means they have combined all four Tenets to create a unique holistic paradigm. This is their claim and they are not lying.

What I believe holistic osteopathic practitioners, the Tenet believers, the Tenets themselves, have done is to fuse the metaphysical with a physical form of holism to form the distinct philosophy.

Though this osteopathic author of holism did not say this and may or may not believe this, he helped me see the actual link of the mystical body, mind, spirit indivisibility to a specific part of the anatomy, then the entire anatomy, the whole, and then subsequently to the entire medical encounter. He helped me see that this is done through the somatic dysfunction and by extension to any other dysfunction in the body. This is the osteopathic distinctiveness. This is huge. The Tenets create a physical-spiritual paradigm. It is generically spiritual and it happens in the body.

I believe the osteopathic tenets create a spiritual link to the body much like a chakra. In yoga, a person opens up their own chakra or spiritual port, whereas in osteopathy, the osteopath opens up a spiritual portal in you the patient. To me, it is as voo-doo-ish as is any holistic mystical/spiritual medical claim.

If it sounds scary, it is which is why it is important to understand.

To start, we have to talk about somatology. One professor of somatology defined somatology as a "philosophical specialty that focuses on anatomy as a source of our belief systems and values."

Somatologists can study topics such as human osteology, human evolution, or primate morphology as part of their work. Some practitioners of alternative medicine may also refer to what they do as somatology. In this sense, the term is used to refer to the study and treatment of the body through the application of techniques such as massage therapy, herbal medicine, acupuncture, and guided imagery. Some people in this branch of the field may focus on providing people with sources of relaxation with some spas and studios referencing somatology in their promotional material.

Practices that are technique driven often fit this category. Osteopathy is technique driven and so much more. It brings the technique into the "whole." Treatment is based on the Tenets. Treatment is based on identifying parts of the anatomy, noting impaired function in conjunction with the "whole."

It becomes a spiritual practice because the person's body, mind, and spirit are not divisible, they are metaphysically whole. The world, the whole is seen through the eyes of the anatomy. The entire worldview has shifted and a new "reality"/paradigm have been created. The whole is a unit unto itself and the whole is complete guided by anatomy with the body as healer and the osteopath as facilitator/medium/portal opener/paradigm creator/exemplar extraordinaire. They are the superhero of God's replacement.

The Osteopath invokes its take on chakras or spiritual points. Osteopathy merely uses words more palatable to the Westerner to create an expanded state. The anatomy/soma, the self-healing body is a source of the belief.

If you expand rational treatment to include blood work and the prescription, all that the osteopath does is metaphysical into the whole. In this paradigm, the osteopath has total power over the patient, their body, mind, and spirit.

The transcendent reality of a person's spirit being incorporated in all rational treatment, including not only the somatic dysfunction but the entire osteopathic encounter, make it a religious practice. If a person's body, mind, and spirit are indivisible, a unit, as stated by the Tenets, then all that the osteopath does is spiritual. In essence, the osteopath is practicing their religion on everyone who comes into their treatment/exam room. The patient, without knowing it, is participating in a religious encounter. Their body is no longer theirs as they give it to the osteopath practitioner as it is being examined holistically.

I don't know about you, but I don't want my personhood seen as the indivisible body, mind, and spirit. I don't want any osteopath linking my medical care, my anatomy, or any medical condition I may have to this paradigm. I want every cell in my body, every weakness, every stubbed toe linked to God, not the osteopathic paradigm.

This is their claim. They "treat" the whole; they see the "whole" because they have the power to do so in this paradigm. They claim it and the quintessential power is in the somatic dysfunction and manipulation techniques. They sense and do not palpate, they open up psychically. One osteopath said that all osteopaths should be, "non-incisive surgeons." They should be able to reach into the "whole." Without God, we are entering into a voo-doo-ish reality. The Osteopath is mandated to see themselves as this to some degree. But more so they are mandated to see you in this way. The spiritual practice takes place in you, the patient. This can become a place of willful manipulation and unholy intent. It has, as you will see later in the book.

There are no osteopathic dental schools to my knowledge, so I will choose this profession to illustrate a point. Imagine three dentists in practice A, B, and C. Dentist A has a private spiritual or philosophical reality. He or she is caring and empathetic, qualities not unique to any one group, race, sex, or religion. Their spirituality spills over into their encounters with you as does their core values. In fact, you spend some time getting to know Dentist A and their value system. If it fits with yours, you stay, if it goes against yours, you leave. You respect Dentist A's right to their beliefs, but they are not yours. Dentist A also respects your right to your belief system. Dentist A does the best he can with the best science that is available. If you need a root canal, you will be cared for according to approved guidelines set forth in the scientific community. You will not however be treated holistically. The novacaine you receive is not given to your whole. You are glad about this. Holism in any form is not a part of their core values. Dentist A has read about it, it makes no sense to him, he doesn't believe in holism. Dentist A is practicing allopathic dentistry, not osteopathic dentistry. Dentist A's dental association makes no claim that they have a spiritual truth. Dentist A's dental association makes no claims that Dentist A has been trained to help you be truly healthy in mind, body, and spirit. Dentist A is not board certified to practice holistically or there to guard your wellness. You are glad of this, you trust your Priest, Rabbi, Iman, or own personal spiritual leader to be your guide.

Dentist B, however, makes the claim that he or she is going to treat you holistically and promises to "strive to help you be truly healthy in body, mind, and spirit." (A quote you found in the *What is a DO?* brochure in the waiting room.) You wonder how dentist B is credentialed to make such a claim. In fact, Dentist B is only allowed by law to practice holistically, proactively treating your body, mind, and spirit. Legally, Dentist B is not allowed to take care of you unless through the lens of four Tenets. You really don't know what this means. The Tenets aren't listed anywhere in plain sight, they are not in the brochure, nor are they are discussed. You like Dentist B, but what if Dentist B is actually expanding your state of being and opening up a realm, a spiritual reality by his or her claim? Dentist B may or may not even realize this, but what if it was done? What if it was invoked by their school, their dental association, and licensing board as they agree to treat you according to the association's rules and Tenets? They boast of being a holistic practitioner and treat you according to policy. They have this authority. The scientifically discovered novacaine that you receive is now given to your whole! What! The science goes into the whole. The science is wed to this paradigm.

You unknowingly gave yourself in your entirety to this paradigm, to Dentist B, and are an expanded state, a spiritual reality. Your tooth is the portal and the body, your substance, is the healer. Your form is reciprocally related to your function so that everything that is done to your tooth has reciprocity. Your earlobe, bladder, liver, cartilage, keratin protein, spleen, and heart are affected and so is your knee. Dentist B would be called an osteopathic dentist. If you like this and agree with this philosophy you stay, if you don't, you go. In fact, your neighbor had gone to Dentist B, believes in the holistic paradigm, and states that his knee pain is cured after his last visit. Your other neighbor, also a holist, however, says that her knee pain is now worse after a visit to Dentist

B. You realize in the holistic paradigm anything can be true. You are starting to realize that physical holism is nonsensical and metaphysical holism is scary.

Now for Dentist C. Dentist C is like Dentist A with a spiritual philosophical reality from which her values flow. Only she is willing to share her beliefs with you if you want. You want to learn more about Dentist C and start up a conversation. Through her witness, she tells you how God is working in her life, where she finds God, and what God means to her. She speaks to you about the love of her life, God. Dentist C approaches you with the belief that you are made in the image and likeness of God. Dentist C is there to serve you as a child of God, a brother or sister, as equals. You belong to God, not Dentist C. Dentist C's dental association makes no spiritual or holistic claims. Dentist C does not own you or claim powers over you or a spiritual realm. You will not be treated holistically; the novacaine you receive is not given to your "whole." Flawed and imperfect, Dentist C recognizes she is not the healer, your body isn't the healer, and your form is not reciprocally related to your function. Dentist C prays that her skill is enough and she follows scientific theory. Dentist C's values flow from the truth that we are made in the image and likeness of God. To her, this is the highest of ideals, moral, and social values of which she strives. Dentist C believes we live in direct relationship with God and treats you as such. Dentist C is an allopathic dentist who has chosen to live her biblical faith in her work. If you like this you stay, if you don't you go.

From A.T. Still to contemporary osteopaths, the attempt has been to deconstruct our current reality, boggle our minds, rid us of our protective boundaries, and create a new "reality" with the osteopath as omnipotent, able to see your "whole," treat your "whole" body, mind, and soul. They are your guardians, not God. The patient just has to submit. This is what the Tenets, the AOA, and NBOME want me and you to do. This insults human integrity (made in the image and likeness of God) and violates the sovereignty of our will. In every osteopathic encounter, by law, there is a submission to their paradigm and belief system. The

Tenets create a ring of submission into a distinct paradigm. They are a loop of beliefs combined with a loop of policies and laws. For me, the only way I could get rid of them was to remove them, to take them off, and never put them on again.

Osteopaths want to change medicine by changing what you and I believe. The AOA and NBOME want me to deconstruct my own reality of who I am and what I believe in the unseen so that I can give in to their created reality. The end game is to have power over another human being's body, mind, and spirit. They claim superpowers when they say they are the guardians of your wellness or can find your Health or treat you holistically. Later in the book, you will see how some osteopaths take this further and give the power held over the patient to animas, entities, forces, energies, and spirits and not to God.

Chapter 3
THE APPEAL PROCESS

Osteopaths think they have the truth.

This was a letter I received August of 2012:

Dear Dr. Melton,
We are concerned about your AOA membership and board certification. Our records indicate that we have not yet received full payment for your 2012-2013 AOA dues and board certification fees(s). Your AOA membership will be suspended if payment is not received by September 30, 2012.
Being an AOA member in good standing is a requirement of AOA board certification, and the Bureau of Membership, under the authority granted to it by the Bureau of Osteopathic Specialist will meet Saturday, December 1, 2012 to consider taking action on suspended members that could result in the inactivation of your board certification.

AOA board certification is offered only to AOA members. My actual Board Certification was valid until December 31, 2015, but was put on an inactive status because I did not pay my membership dues.

The AOA Membership dues were $683.00.

The Certification fee $90.00.

So, it was time for me to start paying up if I wanted to keep my Family Practice Board Certification.

Around that time, I was just starting to understand and articulate the true nature of the Tenets. In fact, I had written an article about the philosophy of A.T. Still and had submitted it to the Journal of the American Osteopathic Association (JAOA). Though accurate, it was not a favorable account of osteopathic philosophy, so, of course, it was rejected. I needed to explain to the AOA membership department why I couldn't join their organization. I started the dialogue with the following statement that was found on their website.

> *The AOA's mission was summarized by its first president: "The reason for the organization are many, are obvious, are strong: and personal protection is the least of these. The primary objects of the organization are, in the broadest sense, to work toward and attain all things that will truly tend to the* **"advancement of Osteopathy," and the rounding of it into its destined proportions as the eternal truth and vital principle of therapeutic science."**

I replied, "This sounds like a religion to me." In response, I was told that the statement was there for historical reasons, but I didn't believe them.

They sent me their Mission Statement: *To advance the distinctive philosophy and practice of osteopathic medicine.* Their Vision Statement: *To be the professional home of all osteopathic physicians.* The reply, "Please let me know if you have any issues related to the mission and vision statements currently in place. I would be happy to discuss this further," started it all and this book. I said I had many concerns that I would be grateful to discuss. I asked if they would spell out the osteopathic philosophy as a start to see if we were on the same page.

I received a one-page memo about the Tenets and the Distinctiveness of the Osteopathic Physician.

I replied remembering my spiritual director's words, "You cannot bring people from zero to sixty in seconds. It takes time." So, I tried to start at the beginning and I tried to start gently. The following is a recap of some of my emails. I have amended them to make this easier to read.

"To start with, I think that the AOA and all concerned would agree that philosophy or what you believe is an important part of life. For example, if I didn't believe that all men were created equal, but believed in a caste system, it would be something that would have a profound effect on me and the way I interacted with others. Cannibals, for example, believe that if they eat another human being, they get their traits, but only the good traits. We might laugh and say, 'But sir, how come you don't get the bad traits?' They would shake their head and say, 'You just don't.' That's the rub."

"So, whenever anyone is speaking to another person about their belief system, each person has to respect [their right to their] belief system. But we all have the right to personally question each other's belief systems. I would like to say that I respect those who believe the tenets of osteopathy, but I don't believe any of them, not a one. Here is why: To start with, the word body has many meanings." I then shared from some internet and book sources about Homer, Plato, Aristotle, the Stoics and Andrew Taylor Still.

"The first time it appeared in literature was at the time of Homer. The word translated is *soma* which means corpse. *Soma* or body was the stuff that we find in the morgue. It has no life. There is a play on words called *soma/sema* which means body/tomb. Later, it came to mean the living body of man, often the whole of his person. There was no separation of body, mind, and spirit." Sounds familiar? Those who critiqued this view stated,

"This implies our sole aim is to exist for ourselves; units worried about only our inner self. This view does not enable a man to get out of himself or to see his neighbor." It is no coincidence that after my spiritual director, a priest and Doctor of Sacred Theology, read the Tenet's, his first words to me were, "The Tenets are a deception, they imply aloneness." We are never alone. "The early Hebrew knew no word for body. The word Adam means literally nation first and then single man second. To a Hebrew, when speaking of man, it meant man in the presence of God. It isn't important if he is close or far away from a perfect specimen of man. Form reciprocally related to function (an osteopathic tenet) doesn't apply if you are viewing man more than a unit but someone who is in the presence of God. To a Hebrew, he is always fleshy, a mere creature, absolutely dependent on God's strength; limited, mortal, and threatened by illness and death."

"For me, I am like the Hebrews. I must be considered primarily not as an individual being complete in myself (a unit), but in my responsibility to God and my relationship to my fellow man." [The Christian pneumonic is JOY, Jesus, Others, You]

"It is no accident in my mind that *soma* or corpse is what an osteopath looks for. My flesh cannot be thought of in any other terms then in my relationship to God. And anyone looking at me for a somatic dysfunction philosophically is looking and trying to have me give my will over to the finite part of myself or death. Soma/corpse separated me from life/God."

"I was made to love and serve God and give, serve, and love others. Medically speaking, the word unit implies that I need no food, no oxygen, and no other human contact. That, like Still's description of how man came to be, shows us his philosophical thinking. Man did it all by himself and doesn't need anything but himself. The body can heal itself."

"In Still's writing he states, **'Man is eternal by his own merits.'** He tells us, 'Man could not be man and not be a wise builder whose powers to select and build have no limit short of perfection. He came to the forest of matter as a master builder and used such material with perfect wisdom. **In him we find no assistance. He alone built his own house**...where he got his power and wisdom is the question whose correct answer we do not know.' This is another off the wall concept from the history of osteopathy. We continue to see the essence of this thought. We made ourselves, we heal ourselves."

"A. T. Still quotes the book of Genesis saying, 'Let us make man,' but Still omits what is written in Holy Writ as he calls the Bible, 'in the image and likeness of ourselves' meaning in the image and likeness of God. In the first tenet Osteopathy calls my body a unit implying alone-ness and removes the most important facet of my life that I am made in the image and likeness of God."

"Emeritus Pope Benedict in a 2004 document said: 'As witness of Scripture, Tradition, and the Magisterium makes clear, the truth that human beings are created in the image of God is at the heart of Christian revelation. This truth was recognized and its broad implication expounded by the Fathers of the Church and by the great scholastic theologians. Today, biblical scholars and theologians join with the Magisterium in reclaiming and reaffirming the doctrine of the imago Dei'."

"Pope Saint John Paul II wrote one hundred and twenty-six encyclicals titled *The Theology of the Body*." [On February 20, 1980 he said, 'The body, and it alone, is capable of making visible what is invisible: the spiritual and the divine. It was created to transfer into the visible reality of the world, the mystery hidden since time immemorial in God, and thus be a sign of it. So in man created in the image of God there was revealed, in a way, the very sacramentality of creation, the sacramentality of the world'. As a

Catholic I cannot define myself, my relationship to God, or my relationship to creation without including that I am *made in the image and likeness of God.*]

"I haven't even gotten to the most important part of the word body. That is what Jesus said, 'This is my body which will be given up for you. When you eat of my body and drink of my blood you will have everlasting life.' When I receive the Eucharistic sacrament, I am living my faith in my body. My whole earthly life, including my corporeal acts, my thinking, and feeling really matter. St. Paul tells us, 'I appeal to you by the mercies of God to present your bodies as a living sacrifice.' Our bodies are where spiritual worship takes place. My spiritual worship takes place in my body, not yours. I change, I grow as I become a tabernacle, and I become love. I don't force my growth on you. Then in a positive experience of dying to myself I will become an oblation of love for others, like Christ's sacrifice on the cross. I treat you as a child of God. St. Paul tells us, 'Do you know that your bodies are members of Christ.' This membership is not a mystical experience. St. Paul tells us, 'You are the body of Christ.'"

"Participation in Christ's body means living by His sacrifice for the world. Christians were martyred for this idea. This is what I believe. This is my faith."

So, you can see from Homer to Plato to the early Hebrew to Jesus to St. Paul to Pope Saint John Paul II, the philosophy of the body takes on many meanings. I do not agree with A. T. Still or the AOA's philosophy of the body, their definition of the person, or their ideas that my form is reciprocally related to my function. In fact, I think the latter is Aryan in essence, harmful and degrading.

I said, "After reading and studying the philosophy of A. T. Still, I can tell you emphatically that I renounce every word. For me it is as easy as renouncing the philosophy of cannibalism. Sincerely, Karen Melton."

After this, they knew I meant business. I didn't know it at the time, but I was engaging in apologetics. I was supporting and giving reasons for my beliefs. They didn't know what to do. No one at the AOA could give me a reason for theirs. They offered me no written evidence to support the Tenets. It really was one-sided. They were mute; they offered me nothing of substance. I got some buzz words, the Tenets, and some interpretation of their Distinctiveness.

After a couple of other back and forth e-mails, I was told I could appeal my case to the AOA Board of Trustees' Appeal Committee. I followed their guidelines, submitted the required documents, a paper was written stating my concerns, and I was allowed to present my case to the Board in July of 2014.

In that time, I had written quite a bit. I was becoming more adept at articulating my beliefs and even more adept at sifting through the osteopathic philosophy. So, I packed myself up, went to Chicago, and sat before a committee and stated my case. I had half an hour to speak. I was terribly nervous; this is what I had prepared to say, though I did not get to it all. I have changed it slightly to make it easier to read.

"My faith in God and my religious beliefs are part of the narrative that I have about who I am and about the world. I believe that I am made in the image and likeness of God and therefore have intrinsic value."

"Through grace, we represent an elite body in the world given the amount of education that we have completed. I hope that you are able to think about the matters that I have brought up without fear or prejudice." [I was trying to say that we have been blessed with gifts, intelligence and education, so let's use them well.]

"We are able to judge, find reason, and truth which I believe is written on our hearts by God. As a person of reason, I look to the authorities of the day. Within the Catholic Church, there exists a body of scholarship that I have sought to help me understand the ontology or the metaphysical nature of the world."

"The word ontology is very important. Let me use it in an example. One student of theology wrote about the ontology or the metaphysical nature of God. In their writing, they showed God to be like us only on top, like a pyramid. This was found to be inconsistent with biblical thought and church teaching. In church teaching, God is ontologically different from us. We cannot even imagine the substance or metaphysical nature of God. Early Hebrews had pages and pages of words for the glory of God. Had this idea of God being like us only on top like a pyramid caught on and accepted it would have changed many aspects of Christianity and future thinking."

"In my heart I agree with the Vatican that God is metaphysically different than me. Biblically in Philippians 2:6, it says, 'Jesus, who though in the form of God, did not count equality with God a thing to be grasped.' So, the bishops had to correct that thinking and point out the theologian's error. Now you can believe what you want, but I chose to believe what the bishops pointed out. Reading this theologian, I would never have picked out the error and it could have affected my relationship with God. Me thinking that God and I share the same DNA, only He in higher form [first of all would be ludicrous and] would affect my relationship with Him, my peace, but especially my ability to accept the gifts He has to give to me. [A higher form of me could not make good on a promise of heaven]. My role as a creature [made, created] and His role as creator would change. This is an important function of the scholarly body of the church."

"Within that scholarship body is a group at the Vatican who study religions, cultures, philosophies, and worldviews. They are the Pontifical Council for Culture and the Pontifical Council for Interreligious Dialogue. In addition to doctrines and dogmas, they look at ontologies (which are metaphysical realms or paradigms) and help explain them. This is for the Catholic, the Christian, scholarship bodies, any faith-based group or religious entity or health care provider. What we believe and think has profound

effects on our daily lives and on our health. We would all agree on this and so would science."

"In a document put out by the Pontifical Council called Jesus Christ the Bearer of the Water of Life, A Christian Reflection on the New Age, the Vatican members look at and explore new religious movements, especially New Age philosophies that are in our culture. In particular they look at the doctrine of 'holism.' ***They compare and contrast new religious movements including New Age philosophies to Christianity and highlight the reasons why Christianity is completely incompatible with new religious movements and New Age thought and practices especially 'holism.'"***

"Holism, the treating of the whole patient and seeing the whole patient, is a worldview and a paradigm that as a Christian I cannot follow. The Pontifical Council tells us that holism is a key concept in the 'new paradigm or shift from the fragmentation of science (the atomos or the smallest particle) into the new age and new religious movements. ***Its claim is to provide a theoretical frame integrating the entire worldview of modern man. They tell us that 'wholeness' is put forth as a central methodological and ontological concept, which is exactly what I have been saying all along, is happening in osteopathy. Osteopathy is a metaphysical or ontological realm of holism."***

"We would all agree that osteopathy is a 'holistic' practice. The philosophy of the AOA Delegates, accepted and promulgated by the AOA as a policy, is based on the ontology or dogma of 'holism.'"

"Osteopathy attempts to make a paradigm shift away from traditional medicine or allopathic medicine into a new paradigm in which the osteopath treats the whole patient. I have given you many examples of this in osteopathic literature. 'We are following motion to its Source; the finite and the infinite into the Whole'. I showed you how it is embedded in the academics of the osteopathic

world, in the tenets themselves. Tenet four tells us that treatment is based on body unity (or wholeness of body, mind, and spirit)."

"From a chapter in Lippincott on the distinctiveness of osteopathic thought and holistic logic to a publication put out by the AOA called 'The Whole Patient', holistic thought prevails."

"I have shown you osteopath after osteopath claiming they treat the whole patient. 'Osteopathy isn't about techniques, it is a way of seeing people and evaluating the whole person, mind, body, spirit, the Lot.'"

"There is nothing about God and the person's relationship to God in the history and physical exam or the conversation. It's all about structure and function. Wholeness is related to structure and function. God is omitted. The patient walks in, you know that they have a body, mind, and spirit and that the osteopathic treatment you give them is treating all parts of them. Voila, you just put them into a metaphysical realm of tides and potencies and body self-healing and with more, voila, you just advanced their spiritual healing."

"A Catholic chaplain may want to know more about the person and their relationship to God. No one wants to hear this part of the inquiry of a Catholic minister, but he questions where are you shutting out God and not letting Him into your life? Where are you sinning? For that is what a sin is. For me, I had to confess that I was referring to the Health, tides, potencies, fulcrums, channeling spirits, altering my level of consciousness, opening up psychically, entering into an unknown and unsubstantiated rhythm called the cranial sacral rhythm and not turning to God."

"If Jesus, though in the form of God, did not count equality with God a thing to be grasped, then all that I did in osteopathy was about me thinking I was equal with God and that I could harness these supernatural forces in order to heal a patient."

"In the Catholic Catechism, the church tells me that all practices of magic or sorcery by which one attempts to tame occult

powers, so as to place them at one's service and have a supernatural power over others, even if this were for the sake of restoring their health, are gravely contrary to the virtue of religion."

"I showed you how osteopathy is attempting to reform or change the old way of thinking into this new way of thinking. From A. T. Still to the AOA first mission statement to round osteopathy into the eternal truth and vital principle of therapeutic science, we see the desire for a paradigm shift and a desire for a power shift to the vital principle, the Health and supernatural forces."

"I have shown you in your own professional journal that the osteopathic profession cannot explain the lack of a unified definition of the osteopath. I have showed you how there is no God in the osteopathic paradigm. The body, not God is the healer."

"Thomas Kuhn, an American historian, sees the paradigm as 'the entire constellation of beliefs, values, techniques, and so on shared by the members of a given community.' Osteopathy is a paradigm wanting its place with the allopathic paradigm or in truer words, wants to replace it. Osteopathic philosophy is a 'holistic' paradigm which is metaphysical and spiritual in nature."

"The Pontifical Council tells us, **When there is a shift from one paradigm to another, it is a question of wholesale transformation of perspective rather than one of gradual development. It is really a revolution, and Kuhn emphasized that competing paradigms are incommensurable and cannot co-exist. So the idea that a paradigm shift in the area of religion and spirituality is simply a new way of stating traditional beliefs misses the point. What is actually going on is a radical change in world—view, which puts into question not only the content but also the fundamental interpretation of the former vision.'"

"So, the osteopathic view puts into question the existence of God and my own worldview. To ask me to follow your worldview or lose my board certification is a violation of my own personal liberty to form a narrative and worldview of my own."

"Holism, treating the whole patient, and seeing the whole patient is a worldview and a paradigm that I as a Christian cannot follow."

"Ontology is the metaphysical nature of existence. Holism, osteopathic wholeness is ontological; it is a metaphysical/spiritual paradigm. Holism is a belief that I cannot adhere to, follow or promote."

"Your worldview is different and incommensurable with my world view and my worldview is incommensurable with your worldview. Your worldview rejects my world view. Unlike the theologian who stated that God was on top of the pyramid, osteopathy has omitted Him."

"Freedom of thought and religion is our most treasured liberty. You cannot force me to believe what you believe and I cannot force you to believe what I believe. Yet, by inactivating my board certification and forcing me to be a member of the AOA, you are trying to do just that."

"I cannot hold onto two paradigms, it is impossible. You are forcing me to think and believe a certain way or lose my livelihood. Board certification is just about a necessity in New York. It affects insurance rates and public perception. I am at the end of my rope, but I will not be coerced into violating my own paradigm and worldview of who I am, what my body is, and how I am to behave in all situations. I look to do what is right and just. I will not go along to get along."

"In the United States, healthcare chaplains (those who give pastoral or spiritual care) have completed over sixteen hundred hours of Clinical Pastoral Education and possess either a Master's in Divinity or a Master's in Theology. According to my dear friend, a board certified chaplain, they are taught the devastating effects on a patient if they do it wrong. This is why they are board certified by one of four certifying bodies and regulated."

"I behave in a way and recognize the authority of the US in credentialing those who deliver pastoral and spiritual care to those in the healthcare field. Osteopathy has skipped this process. Osteopathy is outside of this [state and federal] process."

"In the osteopathic paradigm we see those professing to treat the whole patient, body mind, and spirit through a methodology and a practice of channeling spiritual or energetic forces or looking for metaphysical entities such as the Health, the Potency, the Tide, the Long Tide, and the Dynamic Stillness. The osteopath has combined the spiritual with the medical and there is no credentialing of this authority that the osteopath has claimed."

"You claim a spiritual authority in the healthcare field when you say that you treat the entire person, body, mind, and spirit. As such function in a completely different paradigm. I can refer a patient for counseling and spiritual guidance, but by the state of New York, I cannot give pastoral or spiritual counseling. In my church, I can go for training to be a spiritual director, but not without months of training."

"Osteopathy has no authority in this paradigm. As such, that is another reason why I want Osteopathic Manipulative Therapy, OMT taken off my certificate. I understand that patients have spiritual needs and I will not 'treat' them spiritually with an osteopathic treatment, but do fully intend to utilize the pastoral and spiritual counselors that are available within their faith base. A patient may become confused as to what I can offer them in my practice. Therefore, I want OMT removed from my certificate."

"A representative of NYSOMS (New York State Osteopathic Medical Society) told me in an email that their new mission statement was to include that the osteopath advances the spiritual healing of the patient. Am I to do this by praying over them, putting the whammy on them, or by doing voodoo on them? You are telling me I am to do this through an osteopathic treatment. I can no longer do this, so my certificate shouldn't imply that I can."

"I do not see the whole patient, holism. I see a human person made in the image and likeness of God, and as such cannot practice osteopathy any longer or can I offer this service to a client. I can however offer them pastoral care through one of the many board-certified chaplains that are available in their faith base or if they choose any other religious entity. This is another distinction that needs to be made clear to the public and to the osteopathic student. It was not made clear to me."

"I trust the spiritual/philosophical knowledge and authority of the Pontifical Council for Culture and the Pontifical Council for Interreligious Dialogue. I follow the teaching magisterium of the Catholic Church. I follow biblical truth."

"I do not trust nor will I adhere to a claim of spiritual authority by anyone that treats and sees the 'whole' person. I met the spiritual part of osteopathy in the Health, the Tide, the potency, the soft cloud of knowing, the force that went through me and then the patient, cranial sacral therapy, the cranial impulse, the fluid in the fluids, sensing and not palpating, the somatic dysfunction, and found it to be desolation, despair, a perversion, and a lie."

"Osteopathy tore me down with psychic opening, mystical experiences, loose cognitive styles, magical ideation, expanded states of being, and an introduction into one of the new religious movements, the concept of holism. Four of those just mentioned are included by the coauthor of the DSM IV category Religious and Spiritual Distress as experiences he would classify as spiritually distressing. You may claim this is spiritual healing, but I do not. I'll go with the person in the healthcare field who has a Master's in Theology or Divinity, sixteen hundred clinical hours of pastoral care, and is regulated and held accountable to the federal and state government."

"I am asking you to:
- Grandfather me into the rules where you do not need to be a member of the AOA to be board certified.

- *Give me a personal waiver to membership based on religious beliefs.*
- *Remove OMT from my certificate."*

You can see that I was getting a little tired of all of this. I had been out of the work force for over three years and I really just wanted to get back. I missed my patients, but I could not ignore what I learned to be true.

Osteopaths following osteopathic philosophy really are providing spiritual care in all that they do. Any reasonable treatment by law is spiritual, that is the scope of the practice. This includes the prescription written and the blood pressure taken. Anything done to the patient is done to the whole. This is the claim.

The quintessential treatment, the cornerstone of holism and the osteopathic metaphysical paradigm is the manipulative treatment of the somatic dysfunction. This is what is invoked by osteopaths who claim to be osteopaths.

Weeks later, I got the answer, thumbs down. In their explanation they stated: ***"In her position statement and testimony, Dr. Melton indicated that osteopathic medicine was not consistent with her religious beliefs, but thought that AOA should certify the allopathic aspects of her practice. AOA does not have authority to certify allopathic physicians or osteopathic physicians for allopathic medical practice. The fact that Dr. Melton believes that osteopathic medical practice is not consistent with her religion does not require AOA to change its program of board certification."***

The AOA makes it clear that there are two separate and distinct medical paradigms in the United States, the allopathic encounter and the osteopathic encounter. AOA has no authority to recognize my allopathic training. In fact, all osteopaths should have a sign on their door that says I cannot deliver allopathic care. I am legally allowed only to deliver osteopathic care. This means that I am proactively treating your body, mind, and spirit. They are not divisible. As such all I do to you is spiritual.

The sign should say, "I have in essence touched you spiritually as well as physically by the authority granted to me by the NBOME and the AOA. I have opened up a spiritual realm much like a chakra and expanded your state of being. Furthermore, I have shut out God. I can only believe that you have a body, mind, and spirit. You are not made in the image and likeness of God."

If we had signs like this, speaking up about the osteopathic paradigm, we would not have any patients.

An osteopathic encounter is a religious/spiritual encounter. Thomas Kuhn is correct; two competing paradigms cannot co-exist. The allopathic paradigm does not exist within the osteopathic paradigm. It has been altered. If it wasn't, the AOA would have easily been able to grant my request.

Osteopaths are not allopath's who pay attention to the muscles, bones, and nerves. They are osteopaths and all that entails.

I heard one of the members of my church say, "We cannot love without the Truth. Many want to deconstruct God's truth of how He founded the world. Many want to deconstruct God's love and its fullness." Osteopathic philosophy attempts to deconstruct God and His Kingdom with the Tenets.

Osteopathy is another way of trying to silence the truth and our true identities.

Chapter 4

Holistic Health From a Torah Perspective: Idolatry, Generic Spirituality, Marketing of the Metaphysical

The following is a paper written by Rabbi Leiter. I read part of it to the appeal committee so that they could see that it wasn't just Christian thought that objected to "Holistic Health" claims and New Age Spirituality. This is printed with his permission.

Some Religious Objections to New Age Medical Approaches from a Torah (Jewish) Perspective by Rabbi Noson Shmuel Leiter, Tomim Tih'yeh, Founder, Help Rescue Our Children, Executive Director, Rockland County, NY, C: 845-642-1679
July '14/Tammuz 5774, revised April '19/Nissan 5779

1. Multitudinous Holistic Health approaches, including a panoply of approaches often described as "New Age," have become popular in much of the Western world in recent decades.
2. Many people, of various faith backgrounds, hold sincere, well-grounded, Biblically-based beliefs that run counter to these approaches, approaches that actually extend far beyond health.

3. However, Religious Objectors to a variety of such systems often lack the wherewithal, understanding, and factual knowledge to articulate their theologically based concerns. Nonetheless, those religious objections remain in full force. The very adherence to Judaism, for example, on the part of a given objector, constitutes a well-founded religious objection to anything pagan, for example, regardless of how well the individual objector understands the issues. In fact, the aim of much of Jewish Law is to inculcate Judaism's hallmark zero-tolerance for things pagan, throughout all levels of Jewish society. Thus, even those incapable of articulating specific concerns are to be equipped with the intuitive and attitudinal revulsion for the idolatrous.
4. Clearly, such individuals should not be penalized or discriminated against for their religious adherence, even if not proficient in articulating those concerns. An individual's personal lack of understanding does not provide others license to discriminate against them, denying their religious rights, simply due to their inability to argue or litigate on their own behalf.
5. This brief statement aims to assist in proper and accurate articulation of such religious objections, with a focus on Jewish (i.e., Torah-based) objections.
6. Many of the aforementioned "New Age" approaches and systems hail from the far-East, and are marketed, and adapted by a multitude of individuals, groups, and financial interests to suit the desires of their mostly Western client base. Generally, we employ the hard to define term "New Age" ("N.A.") to include far-Eastern metaphysical systems, the Occult, and paganism (ancient and modern), which are often misrepresented, via pseudoscientific nomenclature, as being scientific, natural, and even "compatible" with biblical faith.

To effectively market to the western customer, proponents of New-Age approaches, especially those related to "Energy Healing," often expend considerable effort employing deceptive

tactics to misrepresent their metaphysical ideology and their religion-related or superstitious techniques as "non-religious," even "scientific," and, commonly, as generically "spiritual."
7. From a Jewish perspective, the primary concerns with most of these systems involve the most serious prohibitions in the Torah, such as the following:

> 1.) First and foremost, "Avodah Zorah," (lit. "Idolatry", herein "A.Z."). A.Z. refers to any devotional practice directed toward anyone or anything other than G-d, the One Exclusive Creator and Manager of the entire universe. Included in this general category of prohibitions of idolatry is the prohibition to deviate from the steadfast acceptance of the Foundational Principles of Faith pertaining to G-d. Specifically, for example, we are obligated to unequivocally reject any diminution in G-d's Absolute Unity. We are also prohibited from any imputing any change, imperfection, or physicality ("corporeality") to G-d. These are examples of "heretical" notions, which we are obligated to sacrifice our lives to reject, if need be. (See, for example, Maimonides, Commentary on Mishna, Sanhedrin, introduction to Ch. 10, Principles 1-5, and end; and his Mishnah Torah, Foundations of Torah, chapter 1.)

The prohibitions against A.Z. and heresy also include the prohibition against improper exposure to, and any acceptance of A.Z./ heresy-related notions and ideas, i.e. ideas that–although not idolatry or heresy proper–could lead one to idolatrous or heretical beliefs.

> 2.) A number of New Age/Holistic health practices, both diagnostic and therapeutic, include unscientific or anti-scientific techniques that are often dangerous, sometimes even fatal. In fact, one of the most influential writers of the "New

Age" movement, Alice A. Bailey, in her "Esoteric Healing", openly warns "energy work" practitioners of the harmful and potentially lethal effects of their "energy-healing" work. Bailey even suggests that "energy healing" practitioners ensure that their clients are also under the responsibility of conventional scientific medical practitioners (apparently, in order to shield the "energy" worker from liability). Any such reckless practice, be it holistic or otherwise, raises a serious objection from a Torah perspective.

3.) Practices which involve misleading patients/ clients about the true nature of the given practice–be it regarding its physical or spiritual aspects–pose another serious objection from the vantage point of Jewish Law: deception and theft. This concern is widespread–perhaps pervasive–throughout the Holistic Health arena, particularly rampant in the New Age milieu, where Informed Consent has perhaps lost its meaning.

4.) Some practitioners involve other religious objections, beyond our scope here.

We mentioned that some techniques, such as 'energy' healing, involve Avodah Zorah (literally foreign devotional service; aka idolatry). How so?

The foundational notion at the root of many far eastern and New Age approaches is the concept of a universal Life force, energy known as Chi, Ki, Qi, Prana, Vital Force, Universal Energy, Bioenergy, Biokinetic Energy et. This notion is based on various ancient metaphysical systems e.g., Taoism (aka Daoism), as interpreted by western (and generally New Age) writers and practitioners.

According to these proponents, these Life-Forces animate ("vivify") the entire universe and all therein, every moment (as we believe the

Almighty does). However, they add a number of beliefs contrary to fundamental of Jewish Faith regarding the Creator, for example:

A. They posit that this "universal energy"–which, again, they consider the Force which animates Creation–is a force within physical bodies. This is heresy, on account of attributing corporeality (aspects of physicality) to G-d, the True Animator of All.
B. This "universal-energy" is subject to change. Change implies imperfection of one state relative to another. Therefore, to describe The Creator in such a manner contradicts the principle that G-d is totally bereft of any imperfection.
C. Man can influence, even control this energy. To assert that about the Almighty is high heresy.

Additionally, unsubstantiated notions merely *related* to this unscientific concept of Vital Life Force would also be included in the religious objections that adherents of Jewish Law maintain, inasmuch as those ideas feed into heretical Life-Force concept.

As mentioned, according to Torah Law, any notion that leads to heresy, even if not heresy proper is prohibited (Mishneh Torah Hil. A.Z. 2:2-3; cf. Sefer HaChinuch 387).

However, in addition to the prohibition against belief in, or even improper exposure to, heretical ideas, merely attributing the effectiveness of a mystical technique to such notions generally prohibits the practice itself.

In other words, IF:
> (a) a practice's effectiveness (real, imagined, or exaggerated) is attributed to heretical or A.Z. notions (be they forces, energies, or otherwise) and IF

(b) we lack a genuine explanation for that "effectiveness"—then it is prohibited to avail oneself to that technique or remedy in the strictest terms (See Babylonian Talmud, 27a, Tos. Shayni;Shulchan ARuch (Code of Jewish Law) Yoreh Daiyoh 155:1; Responsa of Minchas Yitzchak 6:80, p. 112, col.2).

The reason for this prohibition is to prevent people from being misled, by witnessing any "effectiveness" of the mystical technique/remedy, into imagining that the A.Z. element is causative of the said effect. This situation pervades the "Holistic"/New Age arena.

** "New Age Spirituality" **

"New Age Spirituality" is a term that often refers to a prevalent generic "Spirituality- a "Spirituality" (bereft of Biblical morality) in which "everyone" can share.

In truth, however, this Spirituality often turns out to be an informal compact, of sorts—in which all "agree to agree" about NOT actually agreeing about anything of substance, in the true sense of believing in the same principles. Since their views tend to be self-generated, according to their current desires, every individual venerates the divinity of his or own making (often themselves, commonly dubbed "the Divine Within").

Consequently, we can understand that the attendant "Tolerance" so often flaunted by proponents of the feel-good "Spirituality" doesn't actually swell from respect for the belief system of others, but rather from their agreement to reject the very principle of objective Truth.

That explains why their "tolerance" so often rapidly evaporates when exposed to members of faith communities who do accept timeless Biblical principles as immutable moral imperatives and objectively true reality.

Rabbi Noson Shmuel Leiter,

Idolatry, Generic Spirituality, Marketing of the Metaphysical

The focus of the work of Tommim Tih'yeh, for the past two decades, has been to identify idolatrous / pagan/ Avodah Zorah-related concerns that pervade much of the New-Age/ holistic health arena, among other fields, and to unmask the deceptive marketing agenda employed by such practitioners to target various faith communities, including Orthodox communities.

Chapter 5

SCOPE OF PRACTICE: IS OSTEOPATHY A RELIGION?

I have to say that the members of the appeal committee were cordial. It seemed like they were trying to get the point, but there was not enough time. No one could possibly get the depth and understanding that was needed in one hour.

One point was well taken and that was indicated by the response, *"There is no question as to whether there can be a spiritual element within osteopathic medical care. A core tenet of osteopathic medicine is that: 'The body is a unit; the person is a unit of body, mind, and spirit.' The question has been whether that spiritual element is compatible with your own spirituality and Catholic faith."* I should read that every day. That was a great victory.

This was my response to the Appeal Committee:

From: Karen Melton, October 6, 2014
Thank you for your words and answer to my appeal. It has taken me some time to give a response to your decision. I was indeed disappointed with the decision that I received. I cannot be true to the osteopathic philosophy of holism. I was asked, why don't I just ignore it and go my merry way and not practice OMT or osteopathic principles. Many that I know close their eyes put up their

hands and tell me that they can't be bothered with the osteopathic part of what they learned. Their education was a means to an end. But by your own admission in the response, the AOA has only the authority to issue (or baptize or indoctrinate) a person as an osteopath. Whether they practice it or not they are still osteopaths.

The best way that I can explain my desire to remove myself from osteopathy is to give an example. For instance, if a person went to a Baptist University and took courses at the university they would not graduate as a Baptist. Anyone of any faith can take the course work and not be influenced in their soul as conforming to the Baptist faith. This is a good thing. I can attend a Jewish school, a Baptist school and still be a Catholic.

This is not true in the Osteopathic world. I was asked by a member physician, "Have you sought allopathic training? Because allopathic training or certification would allow you what you're requesting in a pathway where the ability to do that would exist. You're asking us to change your certification, CHANGE WHO YOU ARE and make you an MD."

This is true. In the allopathic paradigm I can be a Catholic, or a Buddhist, or an atheist and none of these would conflict with the allopathic philosophy which has science at its core. The scientific principle is universal and in accord with any faith and philosophy. But do you see the difference in the osteopathic paradigm? Who I am changes by the Osteopathic philosophy and beliefs. I am no longer Catholic, because Catholic philosophy and who I am is the complete opposite of osteopathic philosophy and what an osteopath is. Osteopathy doesn't just restate my philosophy or Jewish philosophy or anyone else's it has its own. It is truly distinct. A claim you clearly make.

I explained that in an earlier paper. You can't be a deist and a theist at the same time. You can't be a Hindu Jew. You can be a non-practicing Jew, or a Catholic. You can be a fallen away Jew or Catholic, but you can't be a Catholic/Holist or a Catholic/Deist, or a Catholic/Atheist, or a Catholic/Syncretic, or a Catholic/Satanist. One minute you could be in one paradigm and the next the other, but you can't be in both at the same time. So, if I am an osteopath, I am not a Catholic. If I am practicing osteopathy, I am not practicing Catholicism. This is exhausting, disintegrating spiritually, mentally and physically.

The formation of my personal identity includes my faith and belief in God as the center of all things, not holism and the somatic dysfunction. I AM A CATHOLIC. And the meaning of my being a whole person, of my being fully human is not the osteopathic view. I am fully human when I am in union with God. In my union with God, I am healed. I breathe better, I think clearer, I love more fully. Every cell in my body thrives even though I may struggle. I am integrated into the heavenly kingdom through faith and grace. I thrive by being a Catholic.

Prayer, penance, and sacrifice affect me physically as well as spiritually, as does the Bible that I read and the homily that I listen to. Osteopathic philosophy, holism, affected me physically as well as spiritually, you say so yourselves, only in a very negative way because it is not true. My structure is not reciprocally related to my function. I am not just made of a body, mind, and soul. I am made in the image and likeness of God.

Thomas Kuhn said it perfectly, one paradigm doesn't just restate the other paradigm it is a matter of a wholesale transformation.

You are saying that osteopathic philosophy is great, it is important or why would you be clinging to it. Approaching a person osteopathically affects the person. This is your stance and I am agreeing with you. Treating a patient osteopathically has an effect. It is an effect that I believe is harmful.

This doctor really hit the nail on the head with this question and statement.

I would like to add the following comments at this time. To my knowledge the only way for a DO to become an MD is for the DO to apply to an allopathic medical school and start over. To my knowledge a DO cannot become an MD even if they took all of the MD exams, completed an allopathic residency and was certified by an allopathic board certifying body. Many osteopathic students took the allopathic route as it was called. I did not. I had taken all osteopathic exams, completed an osteopathic residency and was board certified through the AOA. My understanding is that even if I had gone the allopathic route and taken all of my exams allopathically, did an allopathic residency and sat for an allopathic board; I still would be a DO. Would the allopathic route, even just an allopathic residency at this point, allow me to practice allopathically? I do not know. I would still have a degree in osteopathic medicine, not a degree in allopathic medicine. I would still be beholden to the Tenets, the core of being a DO. What initials could I legally put after my name? My concern was that because of the metaphysical/spiritual nature of osteopathy and the osteopathic degree, I was in a sense ordained a DO. I believe that something spiritual was conferred upon me through that degree and was reflected in those initials.

The only real spiritual peace for me was and is to have the words osteopathic removed from my life. I was fifty-six years old at the time of my appeal. Starting over in an allopathic medical school was out of the question. After the appeal, the next step in my mind was to go to the osteopathic college where I received my degree. My intention was to petition them for a change in my diploma. I no longer wanted anything linking me to the osteopathic paradigm. I no longer wanted to be a part of the degree conferred: *Doctor of Osteopathic Medicine*. To me it was a spiritual degree. It was an ordination of sorts into the osteopathic transcendent paradigm. It was and is somehow legally binding me to the osteopathic realm/ religion/spirituality/paradigm. I wanted just the allopathic portion of my training recognized on all paper and legal documents. I was hoping to open a door for others like me to step through and have a legal way to renounce osteopathic metaphysical thought yet keep the allopathic portion of our training. I was also hoping they would offer me a legal way of presenting myself to the public. I never got that far in the process.

Another committee member and physician said, "Well, I guess my question is how are you equating holistic medicine which I think is a very separate thing from anything that's religious?"

I explained that very clearly. The minute that osteopathy defined the person as a unit that has a body, mind, and spirit, and stated that rational treatment is based on this unity it became a spiritual practice. Osteopathy is a spiritual metaphysical paradigm of holism. Osteopathy is a spiritual metaphysical paradigm which is INCOMPATIBLE with Catholicism. Osteopathy is a paradigm in which an identity is formed. You have said so yourselves. Otherwise you would easily be able to grant my request.

In the rebuttal to my statement, one member physician said, "I, too, believe that I was created in God's image..." Hooray for you, you are not an osteopath. Do you see? You cannot believe you are made in the image and likeness of God and believe that you are not. It is one or the other. Osteopathic philosophy doesn't just restate your belief it replaces it. Now what will you do? Will you do like I am doing and try to keep your allopathic training or will you look the other way and go along to get along? Will you keep DO after your name? Will you keep DO after your name if it means that you deny your God? Or will you look deeply into the nature of metaphysics, philosophy and theology and make some important discoveries into the truth and have the courage to speak them out.

This physician continues, "But that also gives us the right of free will and free choice, we're not commanded that we have to behave in a certain way." "We know that a variety of physicians choose to practice as they see fit."

I have to stop here for a moment to state a few facts. First of all, the Tenets are decided upon by the AOA House of Delegates. The AOA then adopts them as policy. According to AOA rules, any member who does not follow policy can lose their membership. So basically, they were telling me to violate AOA policy, practice as I see fit, not in accord with the Tenets, and pay my dues to the AOA so that they can promote the philosophy I find offensive to God.

What I didn't know at the time, and I hope they didn't either, is that the NBOME sets the scope of our practice. The NBOME defines the legal scope of practice and the services we are permitted to supply. Osteopaths are not permitted to practice allopathically, the AOA said so themselves. We cannot supply allopathic care or services to a patient. We are not credentialed to do so. We are only allowed by law to provide osteopathic care. That means that the Tenets are the osteopathic textbook, the osteopathic creed, the osteopathic bible. They were also basically telling me to break the degree that was conferred on me. My diploma says that I have a degree in osteopathic medicine, not a degree in medicine. (I don't know what anyone else's says.) We cannot legally practice as we see fit, just like we cannot drive on the wrong side of the road. We are bound by law and ethics to practice by the degree conferred and as the NBOME sets forth. Like any profession, there is a scope of practice set forth by a licensing board. The NBOME clearly states that I **MUST** approach the patient from the behavioral and philosophical attitude of the Tenets. So, if the NBOME says that my scope of practice is to Fung shui the hemoglobin molecule that is the scope of my practice. So, I hope that the members of the AOA, weren't telling me to break the law.

Someone in the public may want to seek out a physician who does not believe that they are made in the image and likeness of God and believes that the somatic dysfunction, the alignment in their back is the core to their holistic health, and that God has nothing to do with their mitochondria or their muscle spindles or their matter. Crack, crack, pop, pop, you are now whole.

Is Osteopathy a Religion?

I want to respond to the question, "How are you equating holistic medicine from anything that's religious?"

Merriam-Webster defines religion as a cause, principle, or system of beliefs held to with ardor and faith. If we go by that definition, then osteopathy is definitely a religion.

What is the legal definition of a religion?

As I was researching this question, I found an article called *Defining Religion in American Law*. It is a wonderful paper that did a great job of looking at some of the issues related to defining religion in our legal system. A current way is through the United States Internal Revenue Service, the IRS. There are fourteen criteria that the IRS uses to determine if a group is a church, hence a religion.

The author notes that because these are narrowly defined, some of the established religions of our time would not have met these criteria during their earlier phases of growth. So, to be fair to newer growing religions, the author proposes just two criteria for determining if a religion is a religion.

Number one is that participants hold a sincere and deeply held belief in a *transcendent reality*. A transcendent reality is not just a concept, cause or principle, like socialism or communism. The belief has to be a transcendent belief, a belief into the unseen, into the spiritual. Osteopathy boasts of a transcendent belief, the whole person; body, mind and spirit. Secondly, there must be an organization to promote that belief. Not just practice that belief.

Osteopathy meets both criteria. Osteopathic institutions exist to express and promote the philosophy and have as many as they can participate in their belief. They think they have a transcendent truth as does each religion. They think they have a transcendent truth of the person; body, mind, and spirit.

If we look at the IRS criteria, though considered narrow, osteopathy could legally be considered a religion. You make up your own mind.

The IRS criteria

1. A distinct legal existence. **Check.** The NBOME made sure of that.

2. A recognized creed and form of worship. **Check.** The Tenets are the creed with worship taking place in the body with the body and other forces/spirits as healer.

3. A definite and distinct ecclesiastical government. **Check.** The House of Delegates functions as an ecclesiastical government and decides the Tenets.

4. A formal code of doctrine and discipline. **Check.** According to the NBOME, *The Fundamental Osteopathic Medical Competency Domains 2016* document represents expert consensus on the **required** elements and measurable outcomes for seven core competency domains as related to the practice of osteopathic medicine.

5. A distinct religious history. **Check.** We see a history from osteopathy's founder Andrew Taylor Still to William Garner Sutherland, the creator of cranial sacral therapy, to the founder of Biodynamics in the Cranial Field who promote and discuss a transcendent reality. We see the use of religious language from the first AOA president when he stated their mission, "to round osteopathy into the eternal truth and vital principle of therapeutic science."

6. A membership not associated with any other church or denomination. **Check.** The AOA boasts of the distinct philosophy. The distinct philosophy is what separates the osteopath from any other group.

7. An organization of ordained ministers. **Check.** Osteopaths are formed and ordained to open up a transcendent realm. In fact they are licensed to do as such. They are Doctors of Osteopathic Medicine conferred with a degree and title with all the rights

and privileges thereto. If they state they are there to help you be truly healthy in...Spirit, they are functioning as a minister.

8. Ordained ministers selected after completing prescribed studies. **Check.** The chairs of departments, deans, professors, the head of the AOA, are all selected, recruited and required to promote the belief.

9. A literature all its own. **Check.** This includes the Journal of the American Osteopathic Association (JAOA), the Tenets, the founder's writing, and osteopathic text books.

10. Established places of worship. **Check.** The treatment room is where worship takes place.

11. Regular congregations. **Check.** Multiple groups within the profession who meet on a regular basis whose goals are to promote the philosophy.

12. Regular religious services. **Check.** Every time an Osteopath treat's a patient, in every encounter they are practicing a religion if they believe in the philosophy. After all, per the AOA there are, *"more than 100,000 DOs in the US practicing"* [putting into service (my words)] *"their distinct philosophy."*

13. Sunday schools for religious instruction of the young. **Check/maybe**. I don't know about you but twenty-two-year-old medical students are young and impressionable to me.

14. School for the preparation of its ministers. **Check.** There are about forty Osteopathic schools.

To me osteopathy meets most if not all of the IRS criteria, osteopathy is a religion.

Chapter 6

POSSESSION MEDICINE, BIODYNAMICS OF OSTEOPATHY IN THE CRANIAL FIELD (BOCF)

This is tough stuff. This is why I went to my local Senator and read up on the law. One Senator of Albany, New York, has been trying to get some important legislation passed. He has been proposing "The Healthcare Transparency Act." The goal of this act is to hold a healthcare practitioner accountable for their claims. A healthcare practitioner would be in violation of the act if he or she "falsely describes, misstates, or holds out details in their representation of themselves or their education, skills, or expertise." I don't know what was on the mind of the senator when he drafted this act. I don't know if he was concerned about metaphysical claims. But I think it is time to make the AOA and any other healthcare provider accountable, forthcoming, and clear about their mysticism. To quote Rabbi Leiter, New Age proponents (and remember holism is a key concept in New Age religiosities), "often expend considerable effort employing deceptive tactics to misrepresent their... metaphysical ideology."

What follows below is what has prompted me to write this book. It is how I was drawn into what I call, "Possession Medicine" and how I almost lost my mind, my physical well-being, and my eternal soul. The AOA, who endorsed Biodynamics of Osteopathy in the Cranial

Field (BoCF) and BoCF practitioners, need to be held accountable to consumers.

At times, the Members of the Executive Appeal Committee seemed scandalized at what was going on in the BoCF courses. Though they seemed to understand the overt mysticism in cranial sacral therapy, I don't think they wanted to hear about the existence of fluid in the fluid, Tides, potencies, the Breath of Life, etc. in the context of BoCF. One member even said something quite chivalrous about BoCF practitioners, "Give me their names."

I guess it does matter who they are, but what matters more is that BoCF grew under the auspices of the AOA. It had their approval. It grew out of the Tenets. Everything that the founder of BoCF has to say has come from the Tenets and the founder of osteopathy, Andrew Taylor Still. All are forms of holism or monism, which are incompatible with Christianity.

"Every drop knows the Tide."

"We find one Living World, undivided, profoundly ordered BUT SINGULAR."

"We are of one substance, the Breath of Life."

"Healing comes from one substance, the Breath of Life."

"The point of balance is collective; a function of the Whole."

"The whole is the smallest possible division."

"A lesion is seen as a unit of dysfunction involving the Whole person."

"Holism is the totality and indivisibly of a system."

I wrote this to the AOA attorney who was at my appeal and asked him to forward it to the Appeal Committee Members:

July 18, 2016

Dear Colleagues, Administrators, and Friends,

During my residency, I was encouraged by peers and Attending Physicians to take courses called Biodynamics of Osteopathy in the Cranial Field (BoCF).

Many of my peers had met the program founder while he gave a course at the college. I was told that I was at the point in my training where I would benefit from his course work. I was told that it would help me look for the osteopathic primary lesion. My colleagues would talk about a primary lesion and I was chastised that I was unable to find it.

I enrolled in a course, went to New Hampshire and took Phase I of an eight-phase program. A former teacher and mentor happened to be in the class.

The course work was approved by the AOA for Continuing Medical Education (CME) credit. Based on all this encouragement, I proceeded to learn Biodynamics.

I wish that there was a happy ending to this story, but what I found to be the true nature of these courses was astonishing and dangerous.

After several unusual experiences following the treating of patients, I began to question the validity of the practice. I told my patients that I wasn't sure that I was helping them in any way. Some patients had new symptoms of vertigo, one had a terrible panic attack, and one was hospitalized with severe hypotension.

I myself had been admitted to the hospital following a treatment at a BoCF course given at a COM (College of Osteopathic Medicine). We were trying to find the ventricles in the brain. This was a Phase Two course. The colleague "treating" me said that she felt something squishy like cottage cheese. The colleague treating me had completed the course work up to Phase V. She was ahead of me in many ways. She sensed but did not palpate. In Phase Three, *she learned to feel the presence of the Long Tide, the Potency, and the Dynamic Stillness. She had learned to contact the Breath of Life and she had learned to turn the treatment over to these forces and entities. She learned through the course work that they could trans mutate the tissue, saturate the room, and heal. I had one of the worst headaches of my life. I went back to my hotel room, could not lift my head off the pillow, and felt taunted. This experience upset me greatly.*

I was able to return home. I was able to get to work on Monday, but while I was in the clinic training residents and interns, I felt dazed, zombie-like, almost paralyzed. My residents acted quickly and whisked me to the Emergency Room. I was admitted for an atypical migraine. A stroke was ruled out along with a cardiac event. The Neurologist (an MD) asked me about the course. I told him that we were doing a treatment that involved finding the ventricles of the brain. He said, "Even if you can do this why would you want to?" I had no words to explain.

I got better and decided to put this experience behind me. Whatever it was I really didn't want to know. I was determined to continue these courses, though. Everyone seemed to know something I didn't and I wasn't getting it. I took the next Phase and was now up to the point where I was studying things like the Potency, the Dynamic Stillness, and the Long Tide. Again, more unusual things started happening and I decided to take a pause from Biodynamics of Osteopathy.

I was worried about my patients and I was worried about me. During patient treatments, my patients and I felt the "presence" in the room. I felt the room as spiritual. I allowed the treatment to be done by unseen entities as I was taught. I never knew how things were going to turn out. The treatments either went really bad or there was a "high" from them. There definitely was something spiritual about them. There was never any prediction or slightest notion on my part as to the outcome. I truly was giving the treatments over to the forces that are said existed.

If you read the work, these are all the goals of the treatments. The goal is to feel these things, to let in animas, entities, spirits, and forces so that they may heal.

I have enclosed or attached the course booklets. If you read carefully the material, you will find the truth about these courses. They are designed for one thing and that is to let some entity heal the patient.

They are designed for possession experiences. They have never been studied and are not scientific. They are about discernment of spirits, animas, forces, and entities.

I am writing to several of you asking that you take a critical look at this course material.

One ethicist tells us, "The point to keep in mind, with respect to medical ethics, is that unscientific and untested medical treatments do not qualify as ordinary means of preserving health." He goes on to say, "We, therefore, have no moral obligation to use any of these modalities, in fact, the obligation is to abandon them and use tested and demonstrably proven ordinary means of preserving life and health."

The course work that I have attached or enclosed is by no means ordinary. It has never been tested for its validity in any way. We, therefore, do not have any moral obligation to promote these modalities.

In fact, we have the moral obligation to reveal and expose to the public the nature of any osteopathic claim. This is professed in our Code of Ethics and part of our responsibility to society set forth by the House of Delegates of the American Osteopathic Association.

This work clearly is not scientific. It is for the initiated, the believers. You either believe in the Long Tide, the Health, the Dynamic Stillness, the Breath of Life, and the Potency or you don't.

Practitioners then take the initiated, the believer into a mental state readying one's self for an encounter with these forces and then into a possession experience.

In this readying process, the believer's mind is altered through meditative techniques, guided imagery, psychic opening called sensing and not palpating, and group dynamics. He calls it finding the "Natural Mind."

In this way, the believer is then encouraged to break down all their natural and protective boundaries. The believer is asked to give their will over to these forces, energies, powers, intelligences, spirits, and let them do the work that the believer was told would happen. The believer is told that the spirits heal, the Potency is wise, the Breath of Life unerring, and the cerebrospinal fluid intelligent.

The believer is now opened psychically, spiritually, and physically and is ready for the healing experience through possession.

As you read the course work, you will clearly see that the founder and others are promoting forces, entities, intelligences, spirits (the Breath of Life), etc. to gain ownership and control over a person, a patient, and the clinician's mind, body, and soul. This is how the treatments work, through possession.

Possession is defined as having ownership or having control. Spiritual possession is defined as being owned or controlled by unseen forces, spirits, entities, demons, gods, or animas.

Medical possession would be defined as being owned or controlled by animas, unseen forces, spirits, entities, intelligences, demons, gods, or spirit persons for the sake of healing a malady of either body, mind, or spirit, all or a combination thereof.

This is written about over and over again in the course work. The work hinges on possession by one, some, or a combination of entities.

"Do not begin the treatment until you give your will over to the Will of Primary Respiration."

"A Higher Mind is at work."

> "The Potency with a capital 'P' will not appear if the clinician has any desire to control the treatment."
>
> Medical professionals engaging in medical possession practices need to be accountable to their patients, the public, students, and to the osteopathic and medical profession.
>
> As those in leadership positions, I encourage you to do your homework, do your research, critique the material carefully, and identify the content and practice of Biodynamics of Osteopathy in the Cranial Field. I also ask you to make your findings known to the community and society, both of which you state that as a self-regulatory agency you have the moral and ethical duty thereof.
>
> I know that if I had been informed of the nature of these courses, I would have exercised greater caution and would have thought twice about opening myself up to the Potency, the Tide, the Long Tide, the Dynamic Stillness, etc. in order to be possessed by them so that they could heal me and or my patients.
>
> There is no validity to a practice that gives the control over to something unseen, unmeasured, or not tested. Thank you.

Very truly yours,
Karen Melton

This must have been a hard pill for them to swallow. Unlike a view that the effect of a treatment may be perceived as coming from the idolatrous source, I discovered that the effects were just that. The effects were from the sources BoCF practitioners invoked.

A door was opened into the unseen and anything could enter. I am lucky to be alive. There are books on this. Spiritual attachments and true spiritual possessions have been written about in medical literature. I don't want to go into this now, a second book will follow, but it is a very dangerous thing spiritually to do.

I felt that the AOA was culpable in allowing these courses. To the AOA's credit, they have changed their guidelines for CME (Continuing

Medical Education) approval. I hope that it came from my speaking up about these courses. To my knowledge, no other action has been taken. To my knowledge, this is still being taught at the osteopathic college where we were trying to find the ventricles in the brain. To my knowledge, it is still being taught around the country. No black box, no warning label has been issued. I am assuming that adults, children, and babies (yes babies) are still receiving these treatments.

My husband is a very patient man, but when I talk about the osteopathic profession, he gets so angry. Like the Appeal Committee member, his chivalrous side comes out. I know it hurts him and my family because of what I have done as an osteopath in the name of healing. It hurts them to know how I suffered because of osteopathy. As much as I was hurt by being so gullible, my family suffered even more.

What follows is a made-up scenario based on the course work. As made-up as it is, it could have easily been written by a BoCF practitioner or possibly any osteopath.

My husband had to walk out of the room when I read this to him. We don't want to see the people we love taken in by scams, but boy oh boy was I taken in.

Chapter 7

SCAMS AND CULTS, WOLVES IN SHEEP'S CLOTHES

A biodynamic or a holistic osteopathic explanation of what's happening in your body could be like this: *In the body, there are chemical events and processes taking place. Each event involves molecules that have covalent bonds and some with non-covalent bonds. These bonds can lesion and the lesion than becomes a part of the Whole. If the Breath of Life, or the axial fluctuation, or any of the rhythmic forces we feel, cannot pass undiminished through these bonds, there is an imbalance of the system. Our job is to find the fulcrum of the system, the reciprocal tension of the covalent bond. This fulcrum will shift as the person comes deeper and deeper into the fullness, into the Health of the way it was meant to be. We must contact and intention with the Breath of Life and these forces to bring the system back to its original state of Health and Wellness, a place where it always knew it belonged, a place it always seeks.*

I can take that further and tell you that these bonds are different in the bones, in the sutures, in the cranium, in the muscle, in the Whole. It is your job to discern the differences and to then allow the Breath of Life or forces to enter in and trans-mutate the tissue.

Time to fact check:
- The only thing true in this scenario is that there are chemical processes and molecular bonds in our bodies. I made the rest of it up.

- How do I know that there is a reciprocal tension in the covalent bond? How do I know that a bond can lesion? I don't, I just invented it.

- How do I know that I can palpate/sense/intuit this bond? Because I have the skill to do so, because I say so, and because you can't prove I can do this or not. **I now have a power you don't have. I have hidden knowledge.** This was the hook for me. I now had an occult or hidden power. All those above me seemed to know something I didn't. I just could never find it. I always felt like a failure.

- The bonds are different in the cranium then in the sutures. Who knows? I don't know. Would that make for a wonderful experiment? Maybe? But it doesn't give me the right to make these claims in the medical world. It doesn't give me the right to tell the public that if I intentionally invoke the Breath of Life or find the fulcrum in the lesion of the covalent bond, I can heal their malady.

- Does the Breath of Life exist? I said it does, so it must.

- Can the Breath of Life trans-mutate lesions and tissue? How can I possibly know that? Does tissue trans-mutate following a treatment? Who knows?

- I heard one homilist in my church speak about monism (the belief that all is one), which is variant of holism (indivisibility).

He said, "It isn't that the monist believes in nothing, it is that the monist believes in anything." Anything goes in monism. Anything goes in holism. If all is one, if all is indivisible, then anything goes. You can see from the above, a holist can make up anything, state it, and wait around for someone to believe.

Cults, Wolves in Sheep Clothes

I guess the best way to disguise a wolf is to dress it as a sheep. The problem for the wolf is you can always see its teeth.

When I was practicing, doctors from the local osteopathic college came to the hospital to have a meeting. I wasn't there, but I met up with one hospital official afterwards. He told me he found out that osteopathy was in serious trouble. I was the Osteopathic Manipulative Medicine Coordinator at the time and receiving a nice salary. He looked at me and said, "What am I paying you for? This might not be true!" This was around the same time that prominent osteopaths were publicly addressing osteopathic problems. This said one osteopathic educator:

The osteopathic profession is being challenged to demonstrate its unique qualities and thereby justify its existence as an independent institution within American health care. To do so, osteopathic distinctiveness must be identified, measured, and validated. The responsibility to prove osteopathic distinctiveness ultimately belongs to the osteopathic academic community, basic scientists and clinicians alike.

Like my medical school friend, people know inherently that something is amiss within the osteopathic profession. The problem is that no one has been able to identify the anomaly. The anomaly **is** the **philosophy**. It is twisted. It is a deception; it is a wolf in sheep clothes.

I would be proud to be a member of a group of allopathic doctors who specialize in scientifically researching bones, muscles, and nerves. I am not proud to be part of a group that claims that this study includes the metaphysical "whole." I am not proud to be part of a group that opened up a metaphysical door and shut out God. Nor am I proud to be part of a profession that has invented the Health.

If the philosophy and practice is actually a religion, which I think I made a good argument that it is, then could osteopathy possibly be a cult with negative cult traits?

In "Larsen's New Book of Cults," Bob Larsen talks about cults. I was struck by his descriptions. He was describing the anomalies we kind of knew were there but could not name; doctrinal confusion, unquestioning submission, a centralized authority that even structures lifestyle, a hostility if you question the osteopathic premise and a fear of retribution if you do.

Larsen notes some of the things that most cults share in common. I list a few then follow with some facts and some of my personal observations of having been in the profession for twelve years.

1. **A centralized authority that tightly structures both philosophy and lifestyle.** The AOA and the NBOME are clearly that authority. The NBOME has wed the Tenets to a lifestyle. You must approach the patient through the lens of the Tenets, not your own personal spiritual lens.

2. **A "we" versus "them" complex, pitting the supposed superior insights of the group against a hostile outside culture.** You can see in the AOA promotional material they claim superior insights. *We are Doctors of Osteopathy and the way we practice medicine is different, we don't just see patients we see people.* The thing is they haven't lied, they see persons of body, mind, and spirit. They admit that they practice medicine differently. This is different from those who see the person made in the image and likeness of God. They think their way is superior. Any criticism could be considered hostile.

3. **A commitment for each member to proselytize intensively the unconverted.** The AOA is doing this job for all. The AOA

boasts of its one objective; to promote the philosophy. They do this in all arenas; medical, promotional, and political, armed with millions of dollars of membership money.
4. **An entrenched isolationism that divorces the devotee from the realities of the world at large.** I was not given a philosophy course in osteopathic medical school. I did not understand the ramifications of philosophy on the brain, on my attitude, on my emotions, and on my intellect. I was not given a comparative study course on holism nor were the Tenets ever opened up for discussion.

Bob Larsen goes on to describe various forms of "cult-coercion."

1. Absolute Loyalty. Allegiance to the group is demanded and enforced by actual or veiled threats to one's body or eternal spiritual condition or livelihood.

As of July 2018 someone seeking osteopathic board certification no longer has to be a member of the AOA. Some smart lawyers did what I was trying to do in 2014. They found a legal way, (though not related to any religious or spiritual claim that I know of), to stop the AOA practice of tying board certification to AOA membership. *(See, Osteopaths Settle Class Action against American Osteopathic Association, New Jersey Law Journal.)* The AOA was required to pay out millions of dollars because of anti-trust violations related to their practice of coupling of services.

It seems like the wedding/coupling game has been the AOA practice. AOA membership was tied/wed/coupled to board certification. The AOA has tied/wed/coupled the Tenets, four ridiculous, unverifiable and untrue beliefs, to all of our livelihoods and worse to every patient encounter. The Tenets are tied/wed/coupled to everything and anything osteopathic including the patient encounter and the diploma. Allegiance, adherence to the profession is embedded in this coupling of services. If you are buying one you are buying the other. There is no way for the consumer to renounce the spirituality. It's theirs the minute they are treated osteopathically.

2. Financial Involvement. It is financially hard for anyone to leave. I lost my income and what I thought was the opportunity to practice scientific medicine, not belief medicine. Leaving is ridiculously hard especially if you have undergraduate and osteopathic school loans totaling into the hundreds of thousands of dollars.

3. Doctrinal Confusion. A prominent DO quoted in the JAOA said it himself, "The lack of a clear definition of osteopathic medicine... has been labeled the paradox of osteopathy." The Tenets are presented as "truths" and masked with buzz words.

4. Unquestioning Submission. Acceptance of cult practices is achieved by discouraging any questions or natural curiosity that may challenge what the leaders propagate. The big question in school that I heard a few times was, "If the body can heal itself, why do we need doctors?" Or "Doesn't this belief go right out the window when the first person dies?" These were some of my questions to the AOA Appeal Committee members that went unanswered.

Are osteopathic physicians licensed to "sense and not palpate?"

If yes, how is this done? Are they intuitivists? Where would you include this in the history and physical documentation?

Are osteopathic physicians licensed to "entrain" themselves to their patients? Is there an informed consent for this practice? Is there documentation of the meditative state that the practitioner relies on? Is there documentation of the altered state of the patient? Is this legal in the state of New York?

Is psychic opening a part of the training of an osteopathic student?

How are osteopathic students trained to palpate? Are visualization techniques utilized? Is guided imagery? Would that constitute psychic or spiritual opening, if not why?

Does the philosophy of holism go against any other tradition?

Do you have the moral responsibility to inform your patient if it does?

As a patient am I entering into the metaphysical realm of holism as I am being treated by an osteopath? If not, why?

If yes, is this a part of the spiritual 'healing' claimed?

Are you trained by the State of New York to be chaplains?

Are you trained as philosophers or theologians?

How many philosophy courses must an osteopathic student take to understand, body, mind spirit medicine?

If no classes are given to students how do you explain the claim that the osteopath treats the whole patient?

Are no classes needed because the somatic dysfunction is at the core of holistic osteopathic medicine?

In treating a somatic dysfunction is an osteopath treating a patient holistically?

In writing a prescription is an osteopath treating a patient holistically?

If yes, what is the difference then between allopathic doctors writing the same prescription?

Is there a spokesperson for these questions and any other that I might have?

5. Sensory Deprivation. Fatigue coupled with prolonged activity can make one vulnerable to otherwise offensive beliefs and suggestions. I just mentioned the life of a medical student.

6. Hypnotic States. Inducing a highly susceptible state of mind may be accomplished by various means. Sensing and not palpating in OMM (Osteopathic Manipulative Medicine) class, cranial sacral entrainment in OMM lab, and the encouragement of courses by mentors in which hypnotic states are the goal. Psychic opening with exercises like, find a hair in a phone book. All these practices ready the initiated for supernatural experiences.

7. Exclusivity. Those outside the cults are viewed as spiritually inferior, creating an exclusive and self-righteous "we" versus "them" attitude. There is an underlying assumption that everyone else delivering healthcare is inferior. Just look at AOA promotional material.

8. Value Rejection. As the recruit becomes more integrated into the cult, he is encouraged to denounce the values and beliefs of his former life. Why believe that you are made in the image and likeness of God. You can't practice if you do. Why believe in the Kingdom of God, when you can believe in the wellness state. Why believe in dualism, right and wrong, morality and immorality when holism, all is one, is so much better.

Everyone can be fooled. What seems similar on careful inspection is very dissimilar. Even God's elect can be fooled. Before anyone accepts osteopathic thought, a careful review should be made of its premises.

There are many, many resources on cults. People need to recover and move on; they need to heal from psychological manipulation, deceptive forms of authority and control. I think for me, it was realizing that I was being groomed for submission, submission to the Tenets, the AOA, the NBOME, and to spirits.

Conclusion

Though they were cordial, there were some condescending remarks made to me regarding the understanding of my own faith. It was suggested that I go to a certain nun or a certain priest who were both osteopaths. It was suggested I go to the leadership of one of the two universities that were working to establish osteopathic medical schools within Catholic universities. I imagine so that I might get "schooled."

What I never let the AOA members know was that I was in constant contact with a priest who is a Moral Theologian and held the degree Doctor of Sacred Theology. Never once did he tell me that my writings about the Tenets were "off." Never once did he disagree with my assessments and assertions. In fact, as he examined the Tenet's, he debunked them and brought me into a better understanding of the Resurrection and Trinitarian love. I was confident that I was on the right track. I think I kept this from the AOA members because I wanted to protect my priest and my church and not make this their fight. This was my fight. Regardless of my faith background, no one has the right to hold me hostage to their beliefs.

What the AOA has been banking on is that the Tenets are gibberish, hidden and misunderstood. No one is paying attention. "We see the whole person" sounds nice.

Osteopathy would not get my faith community's support if they understood the holistic paradigm and read, "Jesus Christ the Bearer of the Water of Life a Christian Reflection on the New Age," (which comes from the Vatican) or if they studied the Tenets in their entirety. Nuns and priests are like doctors in some way. Each has a specialty and might not be uniformly versed. Our nephrologists can't pass as neurologists, etc. There are moral theologians, biblical scholars, ecclesiastics, etc. The subtleties of the New Age religiosities take some study and not all have had this opportunity. I hope this book opens the door for my faith and all faith communities to study the fallacies of the Tenets.

This is the letter that I wrote:

> *In the Kingdom of God, there are no osteopaths who have false idols and a false spirituality. There is only the truth.*
>
> *So, in essence, for you to be compatible with my religion and beliefs, osteopathy has to be the 'eternal truth and vital principle of therapeutic science.' It has to live in the Kingdom of God and it does not. Though you might be trying so hard, you are a square peg which will never fit unless you become a round peg.*
>
> *In order for that to happen, you need a major overhaul unless you think that the Kingdom of God needs the overhaul. The depth of what needs to be done to osteopathy is ridiculously hard and deep.*
>
> *The Church I belong to describes the Kingdom of God. In that Kingdom, things are done God's way in accordance with His will, His laws, His mercy, His mind, and His love.*
>
> *So, do you think that the mind of God recognizes anyone but Himself as King? So, as an AOA member and promoter of osteopathy, are you saying that God doesn't exist? So, without God who are we?*
>
> *I have no other identity other then I was made in the image and likeness of God, male and female He made them.*
>
> *Osteopathy is a form of self-worship. I am created for the purpose to know love and serve God (not worship myself).*
>
> *What is the purpose of osteopathy, is it to find the Health? That is your mission, that is your goal, and then you think that you can heal people. You and all osteopaths have put yourselves on pedestals. I had you all on that pedestal. But you (we) are nothing*

without conceding that you (we) are made in the image and likeness of God.

I was put on that pedestal for twelve plus years. It is a hard pedestal to get off. But I was open enough to see the idolatrousness and the arrogance of where I had been.

Your outer image looked real nice. But the inner workings of the AOA and osteopathy are corrupt and unholy. That is where I needed to be to hide my real emotions, my real wounds, unforgiveness, selfishness, fear, and anxieties.

In being an osteopath, I never had to come face to face with God. He was shut out. The AOA delegates shut Him out and you and chief counsel sealed the deal by not realizing the gravity and legality of what you were doing. You created a religion, spirituality, a cult, and called it medical. Now you think that because a nun, a priest, and two institutions think that osteopathy is safe and compatible with Christianity that it is.

They are not the final word for me. In the Catholic Church, views, doctrine, and dogma are protected by the teaching magisterium of the Church. Unless I see an Imprimatur or a work done by an ecclesiastical body that says osteopathy is compatible, it is not compatible.

What the Church Fathers recognize is the meaning of every word said and not said in the area of faith, philosophy, morals, and theology.

Because you and I are amateurs at this, you more so then me, doesn't mean a thing.

The fact that you have admitted to me that osteopathy is a spiritual practice is enough.

I want to stop the letter and end the book here. Whether I am stating Christian beliefs accurately or not doesn't matter. They are my beliefs.

Anyone who claims that they are striving to help me become spiritually healthy is claiming that they have the truth, **as does each religion.**

Osteopathy is a religion; that is a fact. Osteopathic philosophy is far from the truth. This is my opinion and part of my freedom of religion, to discern spiritual practices. None of us has to accept a religious or spiritual practice. I have renounced many spiritual practices, as many have renounced mine. This is freedom of thought and freedom of worship.

    I cannot be a part of osteopathic philosophical/spiritual claims. I also cannot be a part of AOA claims which confuse and deceive. I cannot be a holistic spiritual practitioner. According to an Appeal Committee member, I am not alone in this. Many practice as they see fit. **I would like to do this with the legal and proper credentialing.**

To reach me, write a comment or ask a question go to: reform.osteopathy@gmail.com

RESOURCES:

National Board of Osteopathic Medical Examiners
  Fundamental Osteopathic Medical Competency Domains 2016
  Guidelines for Assessment for Osteopathic Medical Licensure
  and the Practice of Osteopathic Medicine

Andrew Taylor Still
  The Philosophy and Mechanical Principles of Osteopathy (1902)
  Hudson Kimberly Publishing Co., Kansas City, Mo.; 1902

Advancing a Traditional View of Osteopathic Medicine through Clinical Practice Journal of the American Osteopathic Association 2005

Pontifical Council for Culture & Pontifical Council for Interreligious Dialogue *Jesus Christ the Bearer of the Water of Life, a Christian Reflection on the "New Age"* January 2013

Defining Religion in American Law
  Bruce J. Casino

Daniela Blei
  The False Promises of Wellness Culture
  JSTOR DAILY-a digital library January 2017

Clementine Prendergast
  How Wellness Became a Secular New Age Religion

Marcia Montenegro
  Wellness: The New Age Trojan horse in Healthcare April 2011

Pius Parsch
: *We are Christ's Body*
Fides Publishers, Inc. 1962
Nihil obstat: Richardus Roche, D.D.
Imprimatur: Archiepiscopus Birmingamiensis

Bob Larsen
: *Larsen's New Book of Cults*
Tyndale House Publishers 1989

Osteopathic Distinctiveness
: Somatic Dysfunction in Osteopathic Family Medicine Written under the auspices of the American College of Osteopathic Family Physicians
Lippincott Williams & Wilkins 2007

"The Healthcare Transparency Act"
: Introduced by Senator Griffo and the people of the State of New York 2013

Spiritual Deceptions in the Church and the Culture: A comprehensive Guide to Discernment
: Moira Noonan OSB, Oblate, Ann Feaster and introduction by Mons. Milivoj Bolobanic author of "An Exorcist Speaks"

Biodynamics of Osteopathy in the Cranial Field Course Books
: *The Emergence of Originality* revised 2003 phase one and two
The Long Tide phase three

American Osteopathic Association
: The Tenets, Osteopathic Distinctiveness And promotional material on their website including the "What is a DO? brochure

American Osteopathic Association Constitution & Bylaws July 2018
: Disciplinary Action: The membership of any member of the Association who, in the opinion of the Executive Committee of the Association, purposely and persistently violates the established policy of the Association or who seeks to undermine the unity of the osteopathic profession or of any of its divisional societies or affiliated organizations may be revoked, suspended, or

placed on probation by action of the Executive Committee of the Association upon the recommendation of the Committee on Membership, after the member has been given notice and an opportunity to be heard before such action is taken. Any individual whose membership has been so revoked, suspended, or placed on probation shall have the right of appeal to the Board of Trustees of the AOA at its next regular meeting, requesting a review of the action of the Executive Committee, and the Board of Trustees, on review, may in its discretion take such action in regard thereto as it deems appropriate.

Tenet's of Osteopathy from the AOA website
  Mind, body, spirit
  Explore the philosophy behind the practice of osteopathic medicine
  DOs are trained to promote the body's natural tendency toward self-healing and health.
  The Tenets of Osteopathic Medicine express the underlying philosophy of osteopathic medicine and were approved by the AOA House of Delegates as policy.
  The body is a unit; the person is a unit of body, mind, and spirit.
  The body is capable of self-regulation, self-healing, and health maintenance.
  Structure and function are reciprocally interrelated.
  Rational treatment is based upon an understanding of the basic principles of body unity, self-regulation, and the interrelationship of structure and function.

The Federation of State Medical Boards of the United States defines 'scope of practice'. It is 'those health care services a physician is authorized to perform by virtue of professional license, registration, or certification.'

www.ingramcontent.com/pod-product-compliance
Ingram Content Group UK Ltd.
Pitfield, Milton Keynes, MK11 3LW, UK
UKHW022221230426
12048UKWH00016BA/988